PRODUCTION AND MARKETING OF MALAYALAM FILM INDUSTRY

PRODUCTION AND MARKETING OF MALAYALAM FILM INDUSTRY

Dr. P.N. Harikumar

Associate Professor & Head, Research &
Post-graduate Department of Commerce & Tourism Management,
Catholicate College, Pathanamthitta, Kerala

Dr. John Major Thomas

Assistant Professor, St. Cyrils College,
Adoor, Pathanamthitta, Kerala.

ABHIJEET PUBLICATIONS

NEW DELHI 1100002

ABHIJEET PUBLICATIONS
4658-A, First Floor, Ambika Bhawan,
21 Ansari Road, New Delhi 110002
Phone: 011-23259444, 65698474
E-mail: abhijeetpublication@gmail.com
www.abhijeetpublications.com

PRODUCTION AND MARKETING OF MALAYALAM FILM INDUSTRY

First Published 2019

ISBN 978-93-88865-31-9

PRINTED IN INDIA

Published by J.K. Singh for Abhijeet Publications, New Delhi-110002, Lasertypeset by Abhijeet Typesetters, New Delhi and Printed at Milan Enterprise, New Delhi..

Preface

Film industry consists of commercial and technological institutions involved in film making i.e. film studios, film production, pre-production, post-production, film directors, actors, film festivals, film crew personnel etc. The demand for the films, produced from Malayalam films industry (popularly known as Mollywood) is increasing day by day, because of the innovations implemented by various parties associated with production and distribution. Since the industry is the fourth biggest film industry in India in terms of movie released each year, it may be considered as an economically viable activity for generation of money among people in the industry. The present study is analytical in nature, which gives a comprehensive picture of the film industry in Kerala. It also analyses the production and marketing problems of faced by producers, distributors and cine exhibitors functioning in Malayalam Film industry.

The study is based on data collected from 113 Producers, 310 Cine Distributors and 360 Cine Exhibitors statistically selected using simple random sampling technique. The data are analyzed based on experience of producers, cine distributors and cine exhibitors in production and distribution, Concentration of Film exhibitors and distributors on the basis of movies exhibited and distributed, type of film produced, operation in production and distribution etc. The tools used for data analysis include F Test, Canonical Discriminant Analysis, One Way ANOVA, Friedman Test and Kruskal-Wallis Test.

The study reveals that production details like nature of production and ownership are associated with culture and political environments prevailing in the industry. The study also describes the production and marketing practices in Malayalam film industry and locates the major problems incidental to such practices. The study identifies twelve major problems faced by producers in production and distribution, five major problems faced by distributors in marketing of films and thirteen major problems faced by cine exhibitors in marketing of films in the industry. Again, these problems vary across the three groups selected ie; Producers, Distributors and Cine Exhibitors. The multiple discriminant function analysis and One Way ANOVA helped to identify the most important problem faced by the producers, distributors and cine exhibitors in Malayalam film industry. As per the opinion of the producers, distributors and cine exhibitors the associations as well as the government fail in providing various production and marketing support for the movies produced and distributed in the Malayalam film industry. The study reveals that Story is the most important element that attracts the viewers in watching movie in theaters followed by Star Cast and Music. The study also shows that Piracy is the most vital problem faced by cine exhibitors concentrating in Malayalam language where as Multiplex is the most important problem faced by cine exhibitors concentrating in other languages. Production problems such as difficulty in obtaining of government grants, cast and crew, focus on stardom, copyright and intellectual property rights, difficulty in identification and obtaining of sources of fund, and visual effects industry are affected more by producers having a production experience ranging between 11-15 years, whereas the marketing problems of film producers such as tax, film certification, multiplex, competition from other entertainment sectors are considered, those producers having a production experience of above 20 years. All these findings are proved by applying sound statistical modelling.

AUTHORS

Contents

Abbreviations

CBFC	Central Board of Film Certification
NDFC	National Film Development Corporation of India
IFFK	International Film Festival of Kerala
DCR	Daily Collection Record
AMMA	Association of Malayalam Movie Artists
VFX	Visual Effects
IFFI	International Film Festival of India
E-Ticketing	Electronic Ticketing
GST	Goods and Services Tax
DTS	Dedicated to Sound
UK	United Kingdom
SGST	State Government Service Tax
UFO Format	Unlead File for Objects
ANOVA	Analysis of Variance
CGST	Central Government Service Tax
USD	United States Dollar
Sig.	Asymptotic Significance
P	Probability
Df	Degree of freedom
US	United States
3D	3-Dimensional
IIFA	International Indian Film Academy Awards
SPSS	Statistical Package for Social Sciences

1

Introduction

1.1 Introduction

Malayalam Cinema, commonly known as Mollywood, is based on the production of movie pictures in Malayalam language. It is the major Indian film industry based in the southern State of Kerala. The industry is the fourth biggest film industry in India in terms of movies released each year. Over the past decades, Malayalam cinema has obtained immense demand all over India, as well as abroad. Malayalam cinema is now performing well in foreign countries such as the United States, Australia, Germany, the UK, middle-east Asia and the Persian Gulf. Even though the Malayalam movies released in India as well as abroad showed excellence in respect of collection and audience response, the producers, distributors and cine exhibitors functioning in the industry are facing enormous problems. The problems faced by them may differ on the basis of the type of films produced, the type of ownership in the production company, the experience of film producers in the production field, the concentration of producers in films in certain languages, the class of theatres in which the distributors and cine exhibitors are focusing, the concentration of film exhibitors in certain languages, the experience of exhibitors in film exhibition, etc. The major production problems encountered by producers functioning in the industry are: Difficulty in obtaining Government Grants, Cast and Crew, Difficulty in Identification and ObtainingSources of Funds, Story, Focus on Stardom, Copyright and Intellectual Property Rights and Visual Effects (VFX) Industry. The major marketing problems faced by them are Piracy, Tax, the restrictions of the CBFC (Central Board of Film Certification), Multiplexes, and Competition from Other Entertainment Sectors. The marketing problems faced by cine distributors which form another major segment in the Malayalam film industry, are Tax, Association, Multiplexes, Competition from other entertainment sectors, Difficulty in obtaining Government Grants etc. On the other hand, Piracy, Ticket prices, Sharing of Profits, Class of Theatre, Digital revolution, E-Ticketing, Theatre Cess Percentage, Promotion Problems, Difficulty in obtaining Government Grants and Difficulty in obtaining Institutional funds are commonly found to aggravate the marketing problems faced by cine exhibitors functioning in the Malayalam film industry. The present study is conducted to understand the major production and marketing problems faced by the Producers, Cine Distributors and Exhibitors functioning in the Malayalam film industry. Since the production and marketing problems are identified as a critical factor in the overall performance of the film industry, it is very relevant to explore how far this aspect influences the producers, distributors and cine exhibitors in managing their business effectively.

1.2 Significance of the Study

Motion pictures today have reached a position of immense importance in society, in all parts of the world. However cinema is even now generally looked upon only as entertainment and its economic and financial aspects are almost ignored. India is one of the largest film producing countries in the world. Film making involves huge investments and generation of employment, and is a major source of revenue to thegovernment.Hugeinvestments are required in all areas of the film industry in establishing theatres, film production, distribution, setting up studios etc. Even though a large number of filmsare produced, the industry cannot be considered a major source of employment in Kerala because a sizeable portion of production activities is often done outside the State.

Film industry is a major source of revenue to the exchequer. In India, the industry has been subjected to a range of taxes—income tax, excise duty, sales tax and entertainment tax. The main source of tax income from the film industry for the government is the entertainment tax. The study aims to examine the film industry and its structure and the laws that hinder, or facilitate its growth. The study also intends to look into the production and marketing problems, to identify the opportunities and threatsconfronting the industry, and to make recommendations on the basis of the conclusions arrived at through the study.

1.3 Scope of the Study

This study is intended to identify and examine the dimensions ofthe film industry of Kerala, and its place in the Indian as well as the world film industry. In the theoretical part of the study, a descriptive method will be used to define the basic concepts of the film industry. The analysis of production problems covers Difficulty in obtaining Government Grants, Cast and Crew, Story, Copyright and Intellectual Property Rights, Difficulty in Identification and Obtaining Sources of Funds andVisual Effects (VFX) Industry. The study of marketing problems covers those related to Piracy, Tax, CBFC (Central Board of Film Certification), Multiplexes and Competition from Other Segments of the Entertainment sector. The empirical part is based on analytical research, where the research instrument is presented through an interview schedule.

The analysis is based on the data collected from producers, distributors and cine exhibitors functioning in the Malayalam film industry. The study identifies the various production and marketing problems faced by producers, distributors and cine exhibitors in Kerala.

1.4 Research Gap

From the review of available literature (contained in Chapter 2), it can be seen that the production and marketing problems in the Malayalam Film Industry form a new area of study, and that the impact of these problems on Producers, Distributors and Cine Exhibitors has not been covered anywhere in earlier studies. Studies have been conducted by scholars in India and abroad on the technique of special effects of cinematography, cinema and censorship, the politics of control in India, movies and mass culture, silent film, Indian popular cinema, etc. So far, no comprehensive study on the production and marketing problems faced by producers, distributors and cine exhibitors, such as tax, association, sharing of profits, difficulty in obtaining government grants, difficulty in obtaining institutional funds, theatre cess percentage, cast and crew, story, copyright and intellectual property rights, piracy, CBFC, multiplexes, ticket prices, etc has not been conducted on the Malayalam film industry. The present study on the topic "Production and Marketing Problems of Malayalam Film Industry" is an attempt in this direction.

1.5 Statement of the Problem

Film industry depends on the co-operation and efforts of the various partiesassociated with production, distribution and exhibition. It involves combining the skillsof artists, writers, musicians, technicians and craftsmen and a high degree of organization and business experience. Thus what emerges from the studio is an art andan industry at the same time.

The producer plays the pivotal role in film production right from the selection of the story, the director, the cast of the film and the technicians, arrangement of the equipment itemsand the sets theshooting, etc., all with an idea of the budget in mind. In fact it is the producer who initiates the whole process, brings together all factors of production, arranges the finance and organizes the entire process and encounters numerous obstacles. Once a film is produced, it has to be marketed. Moreover the success of a film released is dependent on how it will be marketed. The marketing of a film involves the effort of the producer, distributor and exhibitors.

The failure of a film in the box office is mainly due to the poor marketing strategies of the parties involved in the marketing process. Therefore this study aims at evaluating the problems faced by the producers, distributors and cine exhibitors during the production and marketing of films, in respect of the Malayalam film industry.

1.6 Objectives of the Study

The main objectives of the study are:

1) To examine the various production problems faced by producers in Malayalam film industry
2) To analyze the various marketing problems faced by the producers, distributors and exhibitors in Malayalam film industry.
3) To identify the various marketing strategies adopted by the producers, distributors and exhibitors to tackle these problems.
4) To make recommendations on the basis of the findings of the study.

1.7 Hypotheses

1) There is no difference in the production problems

faced by producers who run firms independently or on a partnership basis.

2) There is no difference in the production problems faced by producers who concentrate on Production only/Production and distribution.

3) There is no difference in the methods used by Cine Exhibitors to attract the audience to theatres, in Malayalam film industry

4) There is no difference in the preference of audience about the story of films exhibited by theatres, in Malayalam film industry

5) There is no difference in the marketing problems of Cine Exhibitors who concentrate on films in Malayalam or in other languages.

6) There is no difference in the methods used for promotion of films by the cine distributors in Malayalam film industry.

1.8 Research Methodology

The present study is descriptive and analytical in nature. The study attempts to describe the production details and marketing practices of films produced in Malayalam film industry. It analyses the production and marketing problems of producers, distributors and cine exhibitors functioning in the field of Malayalam film industry.

1.9 Data Source

The study is based on primary data collected from the selected producers, distributors and cine exhibitors functioning in the Malayalam Film industry, by using a structured interview schedule.

1.10 Research Approach

Survey research using a well-structured interview schedule has been adopted for this study.

1.11 Period of Data Collection

A pilot study was conducted among 50 cine exhibitors, selected randomly with an interview schedule for a period of two months, from November 2015 to December 2015. After testing the reliability and fixing the sample size, the final schedule was administered to 80 producers, 310 film distributors and 360 film exhibitors from Malayalam Film industry, from January 2016 to November 2016.

1.12 Research Instrument

A well-structured interview schedule was prepared with the objective of collecting the relevant information relating to production and marketing problems of selected producers, distributors and cine exhibitors functioning in Malayalam film industry. The interview schedule was administered after conducting a pilot study and in consultation with an expert in applied statistics.

1.13 The Population

The population of the study includes all producers, distributors and cine exhibitors functioning in Kerala.

1.14 Sampling Design

Simple Random Sampling has been used for sampleselection.

1.15 Pilot Study

A pilot study was conducted by using the preliminary questionnaire circulated among 50 cine exhibitors. The collected data from 50 respondents were studied in detail with variance reported, to incorporate changes in the preliminary questionnaire. Thus, the reliability analysis was done on the responses pertaining to the marketing problems of cine exhibitors based on 73 statements recorded on a five-point scale. The classical Cronbach Alpha Model for reliability was used. The procedure was started with all the statements considered and by sequentially eliminating those statements whose elimination must improve the Alpha value. The final value obtained for each variable, against the number of statements under this study, is presented in the following Table.

Table 1.1 Cronbach Alpha for the variables selected for the study

Sl.No.	*Variable*	*No of Statements*	*Cronbach's Alpha*
1	Tax	5	*.970*
2	Association	3	*.856*
3	Multiplex	4	*.831*
4	Piracy	6	*.876*
5	Ticket Prices	4	*.763*
6	Sharing of Profits	3	*.909*
7	Class of Theatre	4	*.912*
8	Digital Revolution	4	*.863*
9	E-Ticketing	6	*.794*
10	Theatre Cess Percentage	6	*.744*
11	Promotion Problems	5	*.826*
12	Difficulty in Obtaining Government Grants	8	*.911*
13	Difficulty in Obtaining Institutional Funds	5	*.849*

(Source: Survey data)

1.16 Sample Size

After reliability analysis, the modified data collected from 50 respondents, were studied in detail to identify the extent of variation in the responses. It may be stated that the sample size was proportional to the level of variation and the assumed level of the error of the estimate of the population parameter of the study variable. As many as 174 statements relating to the variables affecting the production and marketing problems of films produced in Malayalam film industry were used for determining the sample size. For an assumed level of five per cent error in the estimates of the means of these 174 responses using the information on variances from the pilot study, the sample size was obtained, based on its response. The formula used is $n \geq {}^{3}(1.96\ s/d)^{2}$. Here, the sample sizeis 'n', the estimate of standard deviationis 's', the standard error of the estimate of the population parameteris 'd', and value 1.96 is the critical value from normal test at 5 per cent level of significance. The calculated sample size of 73 for producers, 303 for distributors, and 353 for cine exhibitors wasthe maximum among the sample sizes obtained from responses from producers, distributors and cine exhibitors to all statements. Hence the sample size was fixed finally for producers, distributors and cine exhibitors as 80, 310 and 360 respectively for the study.

	Population	*Sample*
Producers	113	80
Distributors	904	310
Cine Exhibitors	1156	360

(Source: Film Development Corporation)

1.17 Statistical Methods Used for Analysis

1. F Test

F-test is a statistical test where the test statistic has an F- distributionunder the null hypothesis.In this study, this statistical test has been is used to comparethe of two samples so as to test the hypothesis that the samples have been taken from populations with different variances.

2. Canonical Discriminant Analysis

Canonical Discriminant Analysis is a multivariate dimensionality reduction technique. It investigates differences between groups on the basis of the attributes of the cases, indicating which attributes contribute more to group separation. In this study, this tool is used to identify the most critical problem faced by the film producers and cine exhibitors functioning in Malayalam film industry.

3. One-Way ANOVA

One-way ANOVA is used as a test for differences among at least three or more independent population groups. It is a way to test the equality of three or more means at a time by using variances. In this study, this statistical method is used to test whether there is any difference in the production and marketing problems of film producers functioning in Malayalam film industry.

4. Friedman Test

It is a non-parametric test that is used to compare two or more variables. The lower the mean ranks, it indicates higher will be the preference and vice versa. The ranks assigned by respondents on each variable are averaged and tested inorder to understand whether the mean rank is significant or not. In this project, this statistical technique is used to identify the most important tool used by film distributors for promotion and distribution of movies in Malayalam film industry, and also to identify the most important element that attracts the viewers for watching movies in theatres.

5. Kruskal-Wallis Test

It is a rank based non-parametric test that is used mainly to determine whether there is any statistically significant difference between two or more groups of an independent variable on a continuous or ordinary dependent variable. In this work, this statistical tool is used to identify the most effective promotion tool used by film distributors functioning in Malayalam film industry, and also to identify the most attractive element for viewers in watching movies in theatres.

1.18 Operational Definitions of Concepts

1. Central Board of Film Certification (CBFC)

The Central Board of Film Certification (Censor Board) is a statutory censorship body under the Ministry of Information and Broadcasting,Government of India. Its aim is to regulate the public exhibition of movies under the provisions laid under the Cinematograph Act 1952. Films produced in India can be publicly exhibited only after they are certified by the Board, including television shows. This body is also considered to be one of the most powerful film censor boards in the world due to its strict ways of functioning.

2. Multiplex

A multiplex is a theatre complex with multiple screens within a single complex. These complexes have the capability for exhibiting more than one movie at a time. They are well-designed buildings capable of exhibiting advanced visual effects as well. The largest of these multiplexes are sometimes referred to as megaplexes.

3. *Piracy*

Piracy refers to the unauthorized copying and selling of movies. This copyrighted content is sold in the market at substantially lower rate. The government,of a State as well as the Centre is considering piracy issues as a criminal activity. In India, piracy issues are covered under the Copyright Act 1957.

4. *National Film Development Corporation (NDFC)*

NDFC is a corporation established in 1975 which is functioning under the Ministry of Information and Broadcasting, Government of India, with headquarters in Mumbai. The aim of NDFC is to encourage and develop high quality cinemas in India. It also performs the function of film producing, distributing and financing films.

5. *Road Shows*

A road show is one of the major promotional tools used by film distributors for the promotion of films. In this form of film distribution, the film is exhibited on a limited number cf screens of big cities even before the actual release of the film on large scale. This promotion tool is mainly adopted to create a demand for the film among the audience. Also,this technique helps to understand how the film is accepted by the audience and to make modifications if needed, since the film is not distributed on a large scale.

6. *Creative Banners*

These are also outdoor advertising structures found in high traffic areas. These are mainly displayed to attract the audience on a larger scale. Poster designs are mainly designed by experts in the field, who are appointed by the producer in consultation with the director. These designs are distributed to the distributors for movie promotion. Nowadays flex-type of posters are gaining demand in the market due to low cost and limited time consumption.

7. Events

Events promotion tool simply involves a face-to-face contact between the audience and the distributor in various fairs, sporting events, etc. Here, the distributor usesthe techniques such as free sample tickets, tickets with discount vouchers, etc. Such promotion tools help to build a lasting and powerful brand for the movie in the minds of the audience. The events can also be various conferences, seminars, trade shows, etc. The ultimate aim of the event is to educate the audience about the movie distributed.

8. Guerrilla Marketing

Guerilla Marketing is one of the most prominent promotion tools having immense demand for distributors nowadays. This is an advertisement strategy designed by the distributor, with or without the producer, to promote films with a very low budget. The major investments for creating this promotion tool are high imagination skill, energy and time. This promotion strategy is focused on creating a huge impression about the movie among the audience, for example by creating and circulating a video intentionally about the movie and maximizing the circulation. Some of the variants of guerilla marketing are viral marketing and buzz marketing.

9. Goods and Services Tax (GST)

It is an indirect tax levied on goods and services produced in the country. For movies produced in the country, the Central as well as State governments impose GST in the form of Central Goods and Services Tax and

State Goods and Services Tax. The GST imposed may differ from theatre to theatre and from multiplex to multiplex.

10. Daily Collection Record (DCR)

It is a record maintained by all Cine exhibitors functioning in the country. The record depicts the sale of tickets for each and every movie exhibited in the theatre. It forms a base for the exhibitors, distributors and producers in sharing the profits from movies exhibited and also for the payment of tax and other charges to the government bodies.

1.19 Limitations of the Study

1) The personal biases of the respondents may have crept in due to lack of clear understanding about the statements included in the questionnaire.
2) Clear disclosure of cost details was not made by the producers functioning in the industry.
3) The production and marketing problems identified in this study may not be exhaustive and all-inclusive. But, it may cover all aspects of the problem as far as individual producers, distributors and cine exhibitors are concerned.
4) Research on the film industry has been an unexplored area. Hence the completion of literature review for the study is a herculean task.

1.20 Scheme of Presentation

The thesis is presented in seven chapters:

Chapter 1:Introduction

Chapter 2:Review of Earlier Studies

Chapter 3:Theoretical Framework of the Film Industry

Chapter 4:Production and Marketing Problems of Film Producers in Kerala

Chapter 5:Marketing Problems of Cine Distributors in Kerala

Chapter 6:Marketing Problems of Cine Exhibitors in Kerala

Chapter 7:Summary of Findings, Conclusions and Recommendations.

REFERENCES

[1] Carney Raymond. (1986). *American Vision the Films of Prank Capra,* 271-275.

[2] Gabriel Karem. (2010). *Melodrama and the Nation, Sexual Economies of Bombay Cinema 1970-2000,* 69-88.

[3] Gokulsing Moti & Dissanayake Wimal. (2000). *Indian Popular Cinema- A Narrative of Cultural Change,* Orient Longman Publication, 56-94.

[4] Hood John. (2009). *The Essential Mystery Major Filmmakers of Indian Art Cinema,* 9-15.

[5] Kaur Raminder; & Sinha Ajay. (2000). *Bollywood Popular Indian Cinema through a Transnational Lens,* Sage Publication, New Delhi, 14-18.

[6] Kazmi Fareed. (1999). *The Politics of India's Conventional Cinema,* Sage Publication, New Delhi, 79-87.

[7] Kumar Naresh. (1995). *Indian Cinema Ebbs and Tides,* Har-Anand Publication, New Delhi, 17-23.

[8] Nicholas Bill. (2010). *Engaging Cinema an Introduction to Film Studies,* 150-156.

[9] Park James. (1984). *Learning to Dream the New British Cinema,* Faber and Faber Publishers, London, 53-61.

[10] Rabiger Michael. (2004). *Directing the Documentary,* Panchsheel Garden, 23-68.

[11] SarkarKabita. (1975). *Indian Cinema Today an Analysis,* Sterling Publishers Private Limited, 110-116.

[12] Shingler Martin. (2012). *Star Studio a Critical Guide,* Palgrave Macmillian Publication, 40-47.

[13] Steven Peter. (1985). *Jump Cut Hollywood Politics and Counter Cinema*, 63-68.

[14] Stishova Yelena. (1989). *Look Who's Here: A New Trend in the Soviet Cinemas*, Panchsheel Publishers, 22-46.

[15] Vasudev Aruna. (1978). *Liberty and Licence in the Indian Cinema*, Vikas Publications, 2-10.

[16] Woods Jeanie. (2011). *Vision of Empires and others Imagining Cinemas of Ireland and India, 1910-1962*, 28-36.

2

World Cinema

2.1 History of World Cinema

The history of cinema began in the 1880s, when, *'Roundhay Garden Scene'*, a very shot silent film, was released in the year 1888.The film's cinematography and directions were done by Louis Le Prince. The film is believed to be the oldest surviving film in the world, as noted by the *Guinness Book of Records*. As per the records available, this film couldn't perform well in the box office. A breakthrough for the world cinema was the release of 'Dickson Experimental Sound Film', a movie, which was released in the year 1895, but the actual production work started in the year 1894. This movie was considered as the first experimental sound film in the world. The movie was directed by William Dickson and the running time of the movie was only 17 seconds. Another most significant and revolutionary change that happened in world cinema history was the release of 'Annabelle Butterfly Dance Movie', which was released in the year 1894, a short film. The film was directed jointly by William Kennedy Dickson and William Heise, and was produced by Thomas Edison. The movie is the first colour film in the world, with a running time of 40 seconds. In the year 1896, a film named 'The Kiss', directed by William Heise under the screenplay of John J McNally, was the first film in the world to incite the demand for censorship in films. This was a revolutionary milestone in the history of world cinema. As per the records available, the film was a big blockbuster of that year. In the same year, the world film audience also witnessed the release of the first horror movie in the world. The movie was named *'The Haunted Castle'*, whose direction, screenplay and cinematography were done by Georges Melies. The prominent actors in the movie were Georges Melies, Jehanne and Juleseugene Legris. In the same year itself, the world cinema first witnessed the use of visual effects on the screen, with the release of *'The Vanishing Lady'* movie. The screenplay and direction for the movie were furnished by Georges Melies and was produced by Star Film Company. This movie made a revolutionary change in the history of world cinema, and gave a different visual experience to world audience as well.

In the world cinema history, the use of trailers for promoting movies was first used for the movie,' King John', which was released in the year 1899. This movie was directed jointly by William Kennedy Dicksonn, Herbert Beerbohmm Tree and Walter Pfeffer Dando under the screenplay of William Shakespeare and Herbert Beerbohm. The movie was a huge success and this paved the way for the popular usage of trailers in promoting the movies. A major milestone in the history of world cinema was the release of the movie *'A Trip to the Moon'*, which was released in the year 1902. The movie was directed by Georges Melies and the screenplay for the movie was furnished jointly by Georges Melies, Jules Verne and Gaston Melies. The actual story for the movie was given by HG Wells. Later, in the year 1903, a movie named *'The Great Train Robbery'* under the story of Scott Marble was released. The film was directed and produced by Edwin S. Porter and is considered to be the world's first movie pioneering cinematography and editing. In the same year, itself, a movie named 'The Life and Passion of Jesus Christ' directed byLucien Nonguetand Ferdinand Zecca was released. This movie holds the record for the first colour film produced in the world. The movie also gained much appreciation all over the world.

In the year 1920, world film industry witnessed the debut direction made by a woman director, by directing the movie 'Vampire'. The movie was made on the screenplay of Henrik Galeen and the cinematography for the movie was undertaken by Fritz Arno Wagner and Gunther Krampf. Another breakthrough in world cinema was the release of the movie 'The Jazz Singer'. The movie was directed by Alan Crosland and was produced jointly by Jack Warner and Darryl Zanuck. The story for the movie was given by Samson Raphaelson and was released in the year 1927, and it is considered as the first talkie in world cinema. The movie was also a great blockbuster as well. In the year 1937, the world audience witnessed the release of the first animated feature film named *'Snow White and the Seven Dwarfs'*. It was directed jointly by David Hand, William Cottrell, Wilfred Jackson, Larry Morey, Perce Pearce and Ben Sharpsteen. The movie had a running time of 83 minutes and was a huge blockbuster in America. The world film audience witnessed a revolutionary change with the release of the movie,*'Yankee Doodle Dandy'*, which was released in the year 1942. The movie is the first black and white film converted completely into a colour film. This movie was directed by Michael Curtiz on the story of Robert Buckner. The film was a great success as well. The movie having the most number of sequel chains, is the *'Carry-On'* movie which was released in the year 1958. The movie was directed by Gerald Thomas, with the screenplay by Talbot Rothwell and Norman Hudis, and was produced by Peter Rogers. Later, in the year 1962, the release of *'Dr No'* was another major landmark in the history of world cinema. The movie is the first movie in the James Bond series and was directed by Terence Young. The movie was a great success worldwide and had earned59.5 million USD all over the world. Till date, 23 James Bond movies have been released worldwide and all of them excelled much in the box office too.

Another notable movie to win a unique place in world cinema history was the *'Jaws'* movie, which was released in the year 1975. The movie was directed by Steven Spielberg under the story of Peter Benchley. The movie holds the record for the first movie in the history of world cinema to enter the 100-million-dollar club first. The movie is also considered the first summer blockbuster. The movie 'Jaws' has bagged various awards such as Golden Globe Award for Best Original Score, Academy Award for Best Film Editing, Academy Award for Best Sound Mixing and BAFTA Award for Best Film Music, etc. Another most appreciated movie was the 'Star Wars Episode IV', which was released in the year 1978. The movie was directed by George Lucas and the songs in the movie were given by Binary Sunset and is considered as the first movie to the history of world cinema to use industrial light and magic visual effects merchandising. Later, in the year 1982, a movie named 'Tron', directed by Steven Lisberger, under the screenplay of Charlie Haas, was released. The movie was a breakthrough in the world cinema history, by the utilization of computer animation. The movie has obtained various appreciations worldwide.

Another major milestone in world film industry was the release of the movie *'The Abyss'* in the year 1989. The movie was directed by James Cameron with an initial budget of 69.5 million USD. This movie holds the record for the usage of the first computer-generated three-dimensional (3-D) character on the world silver screen. The movie grossed more than 90 million US dollars from the box office worldwide, and also bagged several awards of international repute including the Academy Award for

Best Visual Effects and Saturn Award for Best Director in the year 1989. Ed Harris and Michael Biehnwere the actors who played the lead in this movie. In the same year, itself, a movie named *'Young Sherlock Homes - the Stained-Glass Knight'* was released under the direction of Barry Levinson. The screenplay for the movie was given by Chris Columbus. The movie was also a grand success. It was the first film in the history of world cinema to use a 100 per cent computerized photo-realistic character. Eight years after the release of *'Tron'* movie, a movie named *'Robocop 2'* was released. The film was directed by Irvin Kershner and was based on the screenplay of Edward Neumeier and Michael Miner. It was the first feature film to use real-time computer graphics in the history of world cinema and the movie excelled much in the box office as well. In the year 1993, world cinema witnessed the make use of photorealistic CG creature in movies. This was made successful by the release of the movie *'Jurassic Park'*. The movie was directed by Steven Spielberg and was produced by Kathleen Kennedy and Gerald R Moran, under the screenplay of Michael Crichton and David Koepp. The movie also holds the record for the first movie using the DTS (Dedicated to Sound) system in world cinema history. The movie was a blockbuster and is also considered as one of the most entertaining movies of all time. The first film in the history of world cinema to be produced with a budget of 100 million dollars was *'True Lies'* which was released in the year 1994. The movie was directed by James Cameron and is considered as one of the greatest blockbusters of all time. The world's first fully digitally animated movie was the *'Toy Story'*, released in the year 1995. The direction of the movie was done by John Lasseter under the screenplay of Joss Whedon, Andrew Stanton, Joel Cohen and Alec Sokolow. The movie has gained much appreciation world-wide. In the same year, itself, a movie named *'Toy story 3D'* under the direction of John Lasseter was released. This movie holds the record for the first film in world film history to be remastered in 3D. The screenplay for this movie was given by Andrew Stantonn, Joel Coohen and Alecc Sokolow. The youngest director to make a professional full-length feature film" was Kishan Shrikanth, by directing the movie *'C/o Footpath (Care of Footpath)'*. The movie depicts the story of an orphaned boy who wants to go to school. The movie gained many appreciations worldwide.

The movie which holds the record for the first 100-crore collection movie worldwide was *'The Titanic'*, which was released in the year 1997. The direction as well as the screenplay for the movie was done by James Cameron. The movie has bagged more than twenty-eight awards of international repute including the Academy Award for the best film, Academy Award for the best director, Academy award for best visual effects, Academy award for the best film editing, etc. The film was also considered as the top best film of all time, by reputed ranking agencies. The movie which holds the record for the most number of awards bagged by a single movie is the *'Kaho na Pyar Hai'* movie, which was released in the year 2002. The film is basically a Hindi movie directed by Rakesh Roshan under the screenplay of Honey Irani, Ravi Kapoor and Sagar Sarhadi. The movie bagged a total of 92 awards including national and international awards of great repute. Another major globally recognized movie was *'The Sky Captain and the World of Tomorrow'*, which was released in the year 2004. The direction work for this movie was done by Kerry Conran and it is also the first film shot with a digital background. The music direction for the movie was done by Edward Shearmur and the songs in the movie have also gained mass recognition among the audience.

Another break-through movie which paved the way for the growth and wide acceptance of 3D movies was the release of the movie *'Avatar'*, which was released in the year 2009. The screenplay, production and direction for the movie were done by James Cameron. The movie has grossed 2.788 billion from the box office, whose production and re-release budget was 247 million. The movie has bagged the record for the most grossing movie around the globe until 2009. The movie won much appreciation from the audience around the globe and was also the first 3D movie to reach $1 billion in collection worldwide. Later, in the year 2011, world cinema witnessed the most expensive movie produced in the industry, and the movie was *'Pirates of the Caribbean: On Stranger Tides'*. The movie was directed by Rob Marshall, with a cost of production of $397 million USD. The movie was also a massive hit worldwide, and was a catalyst for the big-budget films produced later. The most grossing movies of 2012, 2013, 2014, 2015, and 2016 were the *'Avengers'*,*'The Hunger Games: Catching Fire'*,*' Transformers: Age of Extinction'*, *'Star Wars: The Force Awakens'* and *'Captain America: Civil War'* respectively.

2.2 History of Indian Cinema

Indian movie industry comprises various industries based on the various linguistic groups. During the past decades, the Indian film industry has contributed to the flowering of world cinema. Now-a-days, Indian film industry has much acceptance all over the world. The first film released in India was *"Shree Pundalik"*, a silent film in Marathi language, directed by Dadasaheb Torne in 1912. But, some critics argue that it cannot be the first Indian film as it was a photographic recording of a popular Marathi drama. Dadasaheb Phalke, is considered to be the pioneer of Indian cinema for bringing out the first full-length motion picture on the Indian silver screen in the year 1913.The film directed by him was *'Raja Harischandra'*.It was a huge commercial success and it paved the way for more films in India. The Indian movie industry can be divided into various regional film industries based on the languages spoken by the audience. The major prominent Indian film industries are studied in detail in the following pages.

2.2.1 *Hindi Film Industry*

The Hindi film industry based in Bombay is known as "Bollywood". It is the largest and the most powerful industry in film production all over the world. In Indian cinemas, the net box office revenue contributed by this industry is very huge compared to other regional film industries. Bollywood is also one of the biggest film industries in the world in terms of the number of people employed and the number of films produced each year. Hindi cinemas initially explored issues of caste and culture in films, but later socially significant stories also formed the basis for the films produced. A major milestone in the industry was the release of the movie *'Alam Ara'* on 14 March 1931. The movie was directed by ArdeshirIrani and it is considered to be the first Indian sound film. This movie was based on a short play written by Joseph David, and depicted the love story of a prince and a gypsy girl. This movie has also the credit for first song in Indian Cinema. The film was a huge success in the box office also. The songs in the movie had wide acceptance from the audience. The music for this movie was given by Wazir Mohammed Khan.

The first colour film in Indian film history was, the 'Sairandhari' which was released in the year 1931. The movie was directed by V. Shantaram and the story for the film was taken from the Mahabharata. The major actors acted in this movie include Leelaa, Prabhavati, Shakuntalaa, G.R. Manne and Shankarao Bhosle. In the year 1946, *Neecha Nagar* was the first Indian film to win Palme dOr at the Cannes film festival and the movie was directed by Chetan Anand. Another golden feather in the cap of Hindi film industry is the release of *"Do Bigha Zamin"*in 1953. This movie was directed by Bimal Roy, and it bagged the first Filmfare Award for the best film in 1953. Prithviraj Kapoor, Vithall and Zubeiida were the actors who played lead roles in this film. This movie also became a trendsetter for the movies produced later in the industry.

Another breakthrough in the industry was the release of the movie *Mother India* in 1957, this was the first movie submitted from the industry for the Oscars, in the best foreign language film category. This film was directed and produced by Mehaboob Khann. The movie excelled in the box office as well. The first Indian film to earn five crores at the box office was *Mughal E Azam*, directed by Asif in the year 1960. Another landmark cinema Hindi was "*Sholay*" in 1975. The movie was directed by Ramesh Sippy and the screenplay for the movie was given by Salim Khan and Javed Akhtar. Dharmendra, Amitabh Bachchan, Jaya Bhaduri and Hema Malini were the actors who played leading roles in the movie. The movie combines the elements of a popular film and a masala film. This film is considered as India's first "curry" western, and one of the most-loved hits of all time. *Sholay* combined songs, romance, tragedy and violence. The story revolves around the tale of two crooks helping a policeman who got crippled and whose family was destroyed by a notorious gangster. This film also holds the record for the first 70 mm film which was shot completely in India; also, it was the first Indian movie to enter a 15-crore club in collection.

In the year 1982, the Indian cinema showed excellence by bagging the first Oscar for the Best Costume Design by Bhanu Athaiya for the Movie *Gandhi*. In 1989, the industry had witnessed the rise of a new star Salman Khan through the movie *'Maine Pyar Kiya'*. The film performed well in the box office. With the success of this movie, the industry once again revived the romance genre in the Hindi film industry. Another major breakthrough in the industry was the release of Shahrukh Khan starred *'Dilwale Dulhania Le Jayenge'* in 1995. This movie holds the record for the longest running movie in the Indian movie history and it bagged ten Filmfare awards, one Star Screen award and one national award of that year. Another milestone moviefrom Bollywood was *'Kuch Kuch Hota Hai'* released in 1998. The screenplay and direction of the movie were done by Karan Johar and starred by Sharukh Khan and Kajol in lead roles. The movie holds the record for the first Indian movie to enter the top ten cinemas of the United Kingdom. Another much accepted movie of 2001 was *'Dil Chahta Hai'*, directed by Farhan Akthar. The movie depicts the relationship of three friends was much outstanding, and it also bagged the National award for the best film and IIFA award of that year. The music direction for the movie was done by Shankar Mahadevan, Ehsaan Norani, and Loy Mendonsa. The music also was a viral hit among the audience of that period.

In the year 2002 *'Lagaan: Once Upon a Time in India'* movie directed by Ashutosh Gowrikar was the first movie from India selected for the final round of the Oscar Award for the Best Foreign Language Film. Aamir Khan and Gracyy Singh were the actors who played the lead roles in this movie. British actors Rachel Shelley and Paul Blackthore, also performed their supporting roles excellently. The movie was a trend-setter in the Bollywood film industry. After 2002, there was a drastic increase in the box office collections. In India as well as from abroad Hindi cinemas showed much excellence. The *'Ghajini'* movie which was released in 2008, written and directed by AR Murugadoss, was the first Indian movie to enter a 100 crore club. The music for this movie was given by A.R Rahman. The story as well as the songs of this movie gained much acceptance from the audience. Aamir Khan, Asin and Jiah Khan played the lead roles in this movie. Another landmark in Bollywood film industry was the release of *'Three Idots'* and *'PK'*. The movies holds the record for the first Indian movie which crossed 200 crores and 300 crores in collectionrespectively. Both the movies were directed by Rajkumar Hirani and produced by Vidhu Vinod Chopra. Till date, 55 Bollywood movies entered the 100-crore club in collection topped by *'Bahubali 2'* the conclusion, which opened a new record of 1000 crore collection worldwide. But some critics argue that the movie cannot be considered as the highest grossing movie in the industry, since it was a dubbed version of a Telugu cinema released in the year 2017.

2.2.2 Telugu Film Industry

Telugu film industry based in Hyderabad is known as the Tollywood. It is one of the most important segments of the Indian film industry, based on the production of movie pictures in the Telugu language. The industry is one of the largest and the most powerful industry in film production in India in terms of the number of films produced and the number of people employed every year. In several years, the number of films produced in Tollywood exceeded the number of films produced in Bollywood. In Indian cinemas, the proportion of net box office revenue contributed by this industry is very huge. Raghupathi Venkaiah Naidu is considered as the pioneer of Telugu cinema for bringing out the first full length motion picture on the Telugu silver screen. The film directed by him was *'Anusha Adusumalli'* of the year 1921, a silent movie. The film was a huge commercial success and it paved the way for more such films in Telugu. Another remarkable achievement in the industry was the release of *'Bhakta Prahlada'* movie in the year 1932. The movie was directed by Kalidas, based on the story of Narasimha and Prahladaa in Hindu mythology. The movie was produced by HM Reddy, who worked as an assistant director for the first Indian talkie movie, *'Alam Ara'*.

Another notable film fromTollywood was *Patala Bhairavi*, released in the year 1951. This film was the first south Indian film premiered at the first India International Film Festival at Mumbai in 1952. The industry also holds various records, nationally. It was in Tollywood that the first film studio in South India was established. The studio was named Durga Cinetone, which was constructed by Nidamarthi Surayyain Rajahmundry, Andhra Pradesh, in the year 1936. The world renowned Ramoji Film City and Prasads IMAX are located in this industry. The film city holds the Guinness World Record for the largest movie studio complex in the world and Prasads IMAX holds the record for one of the largest 3D IMAX screens in the world, is also located in this industry. Another widely appreciated movie in the industry was the '*Rudhramadevi*', directed by Gunasekhar. The movie is the first 3D historical film in India. The screenplay for this movie was given by Raagini Guna Gunasekhar, Neelima Guna and Yukthamukhi. The movie depicted the life story of Rudrama Devi, one of the rulers of the Kakatiyaa dynasty. Another greatly appreciated movie was '*Dookudu*', directed by Srinu Vaitla, starring Mahesh Babu and Samantha in lead roles. It was cited by *The Los Angeles Times* newspaper as "The biggest hit you've never heard of". The film which collected more than 1 billion worldwide, is considered as one of the highest grossing movie of 2011 in Telugu cinema. The film had also bagged 7 Nandi Awards, 6 Filmfare Awards, 8 SIIMA Awards and 8 CineMAA Awards.

Another remarkable landmark in the industry was the release of the movie '*Baahubali the conclusion*' movie in year 2017. The screenplay for the movie was given by K. V. Vijayendra Prasad and was directed by the veteran SS Rajamouli. The movie holds the record for the highest grossing Indian movie, globally,andopened and entered a 1000 crore club in collection, worldwide.

2.2.3 Kannada Film Industry

Kannada film industry is a part of the Indian film industry where motion pictures in Kannada language are produced. Compared to other film industries of South India, the net box office revenue contributed by this industry to Indian movie industry is very small. Initially, Kannada cinemas explored issues of caste and culture in films, but later socially significant stories also formed the basis for the films produced. Around 950 screens are available for the industry for screening movies in the State of Karnataka. However, certain movies are released abroad as well. Yaragudipati Varada Rao is considered as the pioneer of Kannada cinema for bringing out the first full-length motion picture on the Kannada silver screen.The film directed by him was *'Sati Sulochanain'*, a silent movie released in 1934. The screenplay for this movie was given by BellaveNarahariShastri based on The Ramayana by Valmiki. The film was a huge commercial success and this movie paved the way for more such films in the Kannada.A great breakthrough in the industry was the release of *'BedaraKannappa'* in the year 1954. This was the first Kannada movie which completed 365 days in the theatre. The movie was directed by HLN Simha, based on the screenplay of G.V Iyer. This movie was also the first Kannada film to bag a national award.

Another notable film in the industry was *'Kitturu Chennamma'*. The movie was released inthe year 1961 and was directed and produced by BRP Anthulu. This movie broke the collection records of all previous movies released in the industry. Another movie which won national appreciation to the industry was *'Chandavalliya Thota'* ofthe year 1962. This movie was directed by TV Singh Thakur and the movie is the first Kannada movie to win the President's medal for Best Film. Later the release of the *'Amarashilpi Jakanachari'* movie in the year 1964 was another breakthrough in the industry. It is also the first colour film in Kannada. The film was directed and produced by BindiganavileSrinivasIyengarRangaa and the screenplay for the movie was given by Balasubramanyam. Another much appreciated movie was *'Bangarada Manushya'* released in the year 1972. This movie ran for more than two years and was the highest grossing movie in the industry for a very long time.

The first full fledged commercial children's film was *'Nagara Hole'*, which was released in the year 1977. The film was directed by Rajendra Singh Babu and was produced by Manik Chand, Balaji Singh and SN Parthanath. The film was greatly appreciated by all classes of audience in the industry and was also a top success in the box office. This film paved the way for more movies of that genre in the industry. In the year 2007, the industry witnessed the direction made by a ten-year-old child, Kishan Shrikanth. The movie directed by him was *'C/O Footpath'*. This movie holds the Guinness Record for the youngest child who directed a film at the age of ten. The film also bagged the Best Children's Film Award, two Karnataka State Awards, and eleven International Awards from countries such as Italy, Spain, Greece, Egypt, Qatar, Iran, USA and UK. The Kannada movies suchas *'Vamshavruksha', 'Hamsageethe, Ghatashraddha', 'Ranganayaki', 'Sarovara', 'Dweepa Aptharakshaka', 'Dandupalya', 'Rangi Taranga'*, and *'Killing Veerappan'* have made revolutionary changes in the Kannada film industry.

2.2.4 Tamil Film Industry

The Tamil film industry is a part of the Indian film industry, where motion pictures in Tamil language are produced. It is the film industry based in Madras (now known as Chennai), and is popularly known as the Kollywood. It is one of the fastest growing and prominent film industries of South India. The Madras city once upon a time served as a base for all South Indian films. The industry is also the largest film production centre in south India. R Nataraja Mudaliar is considered as the pioneer of Tamil cinema for bringing out the first full-length motion picture on the Tamil silver screen. The film directed and produced by him was *'KeechakaVadham'* in the year 1918, a silent movie. The screenplay for the movie was given by C Rangavadivelu. The film was a huge commercial success and this movie paved the way for more such films in the Tamil film industry as well as in the south Indian film industry.

A major milestone in the industry was the release of the movie *'Kalidas'* in the year 1931. The film was directed by H M. Reddy and was produced by Ardeshir Irani. The movie is the first Tamil language sound film and also the first sound movie in South India. The movie was based on the life story of the Sanskrit poet, Kalidasa. In the year 1937, the industry witnessed the first children's film in Tamil,*'Balayogini'*, directed and produced by K. Subramanyam, and is also the first movie of such genre in South India. Another remarkable achievement for the industry was that, the Tamil actor Sivaji Ganeshan won the Best Actor award at an International film festival in the year 1960, held at Cairo in Egypt, he also received the President's Award for the Best Tamil Actor twelve times. He also received four South Filmfare Awards, National Film Award, and also the Dadasaheb Phalke Award, the highest honour for films in India.

The first National Award for Best Film in Tamil was won by the movie *'Marupakkam'*, released in the year 1990. The movie was directed by KS Sethu Madhavan and was produced by Indira Parthasarathy, based on the script of Indira Parthasarathy. The movie also bagged the Golden Lotus Award for Best Film of that year. *'Kalathur Kannamma'* movie directed by A Bhim Singh in the year 1959 was another much appreciated movie. The Child Actor in the movie, Kamal Hassan, won the President's

Gold Medal for the Best Child Actor. *'Roja'* movie directed by Mani Ratnam, in the year 1992 was another trend-setter movie in the industry. The debut work made by AR Rahman, the music director in the movie was much appreciated and the movie became a trend setter for the upcoming movie songs in Tamil and Indian film music. The songs in the movie were a massive hit among the audience of that time. The highest budget film produced in the industry was*'Enthiran'*, released in the year 2010. The screenplay and the direction for the movie were done by Shankar and produced by KalanidthiMaran. The movie was a blockbuster in the box office.It was awarded two Indian National Film Awards, three Filmfare Awards, seven Vijay Awards and two Screen Awards. Rajnikanth, who played the lead role in the film is considered as one of the major Superstars of this industry and is also the highest-paid actor in Asia after Jackie Chan. Several Tamil films have proved excellence at the international level. The notable movies include *'Kannathil Muthamittal'* directed by Mani Ratnam, *'Kanchivaram'* movie directed by Priyadarshan, and *'Paruthiveeran'* directed by Ameer Sultan.

2.2.5 Konkani Film Industry

The Konkani film industry is a part of the Indian film industry,where motion pictures in Konkani language are produced. The language is spoken mainly in the Indian States of Goa, Maharashtra and Karnataka and in smaller parts of Kerala. Since a great number of Konkani-speaking people are residing in the state of Karnataka, the state is considered as a central hub for Konkani film industry. The first full-length Konkani film was *'Sukhi Konn'*, produced by GMB Rodrigues in the year 1949, but due to several issues the film couldn't be screened before the audience. One year after the release of *'Sukhi Konn'*, a movie named *'Mogacho Anvddo'* was released. The movie was produced and directed by Jerry Braganza, under the banner of ETICA Pictures. Hence, the release date of this movie, 24 April, is celebrated as the Konkani Film Day.

A major milestone in the industry was the release of the movie *'Nirmonn'* in the year 1966. The movie was directed and produced by A Salim and Franklin Fernandes respectively. The film was the first Konkani movie to win a national award. Another notable film released in the industry was the *'Mog and Moipass'*, released in the year 1977 and is the first colour film in Konkani. The film was a huge success in the box office as well. Later, in the year, 2004 and 2006, the Konkani movies excelled much at the national level. The movie *'Aleesha'* wasreleased in the year 2004, and*'Antarnad'*in the year 2006, both directed and produced by RajendraTalakwon. These films won the best feature movie in Konkani, in the 52nd National Film Awards and 59th National Film Awards respectively. Another film which gained international repute was *'Tum KitemKortoloAslo'* movie, directed and produced by Sharon Mazarello. The film was selected for screening at Addis Ababa international film festival and Marbella International Film Festival. *'Baga Beach'* movie directed by Laxmikant Shetgaonkar and produced by Pramod Salgaocar was screened at International Film Festival of India and won a national award in the year 2013. The first Children's film fromKonkani was *'AaVaiJa Sa'* which was released in the year 2016. The film was produced by Ramesh Kamath.

2.2.6 Bengali Film Industry

The Bengali film industry is a part of the Indian film industry, where motion pictures in Bengali language are produced. It is the film industry based in Kolkata, West Bengal, and is popularly known as the Gollywood. When compared to other, film industries in India, such as Bollywood, Telugu cinema, Tamil cinema and Malayalam cinema, the number of films produced each year and the number of people employed ever year in the industry are comparatively small. However, the industry is very popular globally for making some of the most critically acclaimed Indian movies including art films. 'Rustomji Dhotiwala' is considered as the pioneer of Bengali cinema, for bringing out the first full-length motion picture on the Bengali silver screen.The film directed by him was a silent film *'Satyawadi Raja Harishchandra'*, and was produced by Elphinstone Bioscope.The film directed by him was the remake of the first Indian film, *'Raja Harishchandra'* directed by Dadasaheb Phalke, and the movie is also regarded as the first remake of an Indian film.

A major milestone in the industry was the release *'Billwamangal'* movie in the year 1919. The film was directed by Rustomji Dhotiwala, with the screenplay of Champsi Udeshi. The film is considered as the first Bengali Feature film. But the industry had to wait for several years for producing and screening, the first talkie in Bengali language. In the year 1931, the first Bengali talkie, *'Jamai Shashthi'*, was released. The film was directed by Amar Choudhury and was produced by Madan Theatre Limited. The film was a huge success in the box office as well. Another most globally appreciated movie from the industry was *'Pather Panchali'*. The film was released is the year 1955, under the debut direction by Satyajit Ray and was produced by the West Bengal government. The movie is considered as one of the major turning points in Indian cinema history. This movie is considered as one of the major movies that pioneered the Parallel Cinema movement, which espoused social realism on the screen. This was also the first film from India to attract a global critical attention. The film also bagged India's National Film Award for Best Feature Film in the year 1955 and Best Human Document award of the year 1956 at Cannes Film Festival. Ray was also the recipient of India's greatest civilian honour, Bharat Ratna, and France's greatest civilian honour, Legion of Honor.

Another major movie released in the industry was *'Rajat Jayanti'*. The movie was released in the year 1939, and was directed by PramatheshBarua under the banner of New Theatres Private Limited. This movie is considered as the first Bengali comedy film. This film very well excelled in the box office. During the past decades, the industry captured a major proportion of the audience in the states of Tripura, Assam and also in the country of Bangladesh as well. The classic Bengali films such as *'Nagarik',' The Apu Trilogy', 'Jalsaghar, Ajantrik',' Neel AkasherNeechey', 'Devdas, Devi', 'Meghe Dhaka Tara', 'the Calcutta trilogies'* etc are considered as some of the greatest Bengali films of all time.

2.2.7 Punjabi Film Industry

The Punjabi film industry is a part of the Indian film industry, where motion pictures in Punjabi language are produced. It is the film industry based on Punjab and is popularly known asPollywood. KD Mehra is considered as the pioneer of Punjabi cinema, for bringing out the first full length motion picture on the Punjabi silver screen, *'Sheela'*. The film was also the first talkie in Punjabi and was produced by Indira Movietone, in the year 1935. The film was very successful in the box office as well. After the success of the movie *'Sheela'*, Metha made his second film,*'Heer Syal'*, based on the screenplay of F.D Sharaff. The movie was produced by IndraMovitone. The movie was also a great success. One of the major releases in the industry was the release of *'Pehchaan'* 3D movie in the year 2013. The movie was directed by Manny Parmarbased on the screenplayof Gurpreet Sohi, Gurdip Bhullaar, Namrit Uppaal and Navtej Jassar. The movie was the first 3D Punjabi film.

The first Punjabi film that achieved international repute was *'Anhe Ghore Da Daan'*, which was released in the year 2012. The direction of the movie was made by Gurvinder

Singh, based on the story of Gurdial Singh. The film was produced by theNational Film Development Corporation of India. It was the first Punjabi movieselected for screening in international film festivals. The film was premiered at the 68th Venice International Film Festival, 55th BFI London Film Festival, 49th New York Film Festival and the 16thBusan International Film Festival. The film also bagged $50,000 Black Pearl trophy at the Abu Dhabi Film Festival, and the Golden Peacock award for the best film at the 43rd International Film Festival of India. The film also bagged the National award for Best Direction, National award for Best Feature Film and the National Film Award for Best Cinematography in the year 2012.

Other major movies which excelled much at the national levels include '*Satluj De Kandhe*', movie which was released in the year 1964 and directed by MM BilloMehra and PPMaheshwary, and '*Nanak Nam JahazHai*' movie, which was released in the year 1969 and directed by Ram Maheshwary. Both the movies won the National Film Award's Certificate of Merit. Another notable movie in the industry was '*Nabar*', which was released in the year 2013, and directed by Rajeev Kumarbased on the story of Balwinder Singh Grewal. It won the National Film Award for Best Feature Film in Punjabi. '*The Punjab 1984*' movie released in the year 2014, directed by Anurag Singh under the Screenplay of Anurag Singh and Surmet Maavi, won the National Film Award for Best Feature Filmin Punjabi at the 60th National Film Awards. Other most appreciated movies inthe industry which won the Best Feature Film awards include '*Jagga (1964)*', '*Sassi Punnu (1964)*', '*Satluj De Kandhe (1967*'), '*Chann Pardesi (1980)*', '*Kachehri (1994)*', '*Main Maa Punjab Dee (1998)*', '*Shaheed-e-Mohabbat Boota Singh (1999)*', '*Shaheed Udham Singh (2000)*', '*Des Hoyaa Pardes (2005)*'and '*Waris Shah: Ishq Daa Waaris (2006)*'.

2.2.8 *Assamese Film Industry*

The Assamese film industry is a part of the Indian film industry, where motion pictures in Assamese language are produced. Jyoti Prasad Agarwalais considered as the pioneer of Assamese cinema, for bringing out the first full length motion picture *'Joymoti'* on the Assam silver screen. The film was released in the year 1935 and was directed and produced by Jyoti Prasad Agarwala based on the screenplay of LakshminathBezbaroa. The film was also the first Indian talkie that used the facility of re-recording and dubbing. The film also obtained various international appreciations as well. It was screened in some of the most prestigious film festivals around the globe, which include the India-Bangladesh Joint Celebration of 100 Years of Indian Cinema, which was held in Dhaka in the year 2012, and Munich Film Festival of 2006. The film was also a huge success in the box office.

Another most appreciated movie produced in the industry was *'Piyali Phukan'* movie which was directed by PhaniSarma under the Rup Jyoti Productions of Gama Prasad Agarwalla. The movie was released in the year 1955 and has bagged the President's Silver Medal for the best film; also the film received a Certificate of Merit from the India Government in the same year itself. Later in the year 1958, a movie named *'Ronga Police'* under the direction of Nip Barua, also obtained the President's Silver Medal for the Best Feature Film in Assamese. The film was produced by Kanak Chandra Sharma. Another landmark film in the industry was *'Adajya'* movie, which was released in the year 1996 under the direction of Santwana Bardoloi. The screenplay for this movie was given by Santwana Bardoloi. The film secured the National Film Award for Best Feature Film in Assamese in the year 1996. Indira Gandhi Award for Best First Film of a Director was bagged by Rag Birag, another golden feature for the industry. The movie was directed by Bidyut Chakraborty under the Cinematography of Mrinalkanti Das. Another major award in the industry is the Prag Cine Awards, presented annually by Prag News. The aim of awarding this prize is to give an inspiration to the Assamese film industry; it is awarded in honour of the personalities who contributed to the film industry. A major film festival common in the North eastern states of India is the Brahmaputra Valley Film Festival. It is a new and innovative initiative for new film makers in the industry to create and rediscover various aspects of film making. This film festival is hosted in Guwahati, annually, since 2013.

2.2.9 Manipuri Film Industry

The Manipuri film industry is a part of the Indian film industry, where motion pictures in Manipuri language are produced. It is the film industry based on, Manipurand is popularly known as the Maniwood. When compared to other film industries of north east India, the net box office revenue contributed by this industry to Indian movie industry is very small. Debkumar Bose is considered as the pioneer of Manipuri cinema for bringing out the first full-length motion picture in the Manipuri silver screen. The film directed by him was *'Matamgi Manipur'*. The film was released in the year 1972 and is considered as the first Manipuri feature film. The film also won the Best Feature Film Award in Manipuri Language at the 20th National Film Awards. Another major landmark in the history of the industry was the *'Langlen Thadoi'*, which was released in the year 1984. The movie was directed by MA Singh and is considered as the first colour film in Manipur film industry.

Another notable movie that gained international recognition was *'Ishanou'* movie, directed by Aribam Syam Sharma based on the screenplay of Binodini Devi. The movie was released in the year 1990, and was selected for screening at the Cannes International Film Festival.

In the year 2007, *'Yenning Amadi Likla'*, a movie directed by Mankhonmani Mongsaba on the screenplay of Moirangthem Inao, got an entry into the feature film section of the Indian Panorama of the International Film Festival of India (IFFI) 2007. This was another major golden feature ofthe industry. In later years, also the industry had a significant role in the international arena. Another film from the industry which excelled much in the international film festival is *'Leipaklei'*, which was released in the year 2012. The film was directed and produced by Aribam Syam Sharma. The film was selected for screening at the Jeonju International Film Festival 2012,18th Kolkata International Film Festival, and 5th Guwahati Film Festival. Also films such as *'Nangna Kappa Pakchade'* and *'Nongmatang'* directed by Mankhonmani Mongsaba and Suvas respectively, were selected for screening at the 3rd Delhi InternationalFilm Festival.

2.2.10 Gujarati Film Industry

The Gujarati film industry is a part of the Indian film industry, where motion pictures in Gujarati language are produced. It is the film industry based in Gujarat and is popularly known as Gollywood. A major landmark film in the industry was the release of the movie *'Narsinh Mehta'* in the year 1932.The film was produced by Chimanbhai Desai and was directed by Nanubhai Vakil based on the screenplay of Chaturbhuj Doshi. The movie was the first talkie film in the industry. The release of the movie marked an actual beginning of Gujarati cinema. Another movie which made a breakthrough in the industry was*'Sonbaini Chundadi'*, which was released in the year 1976.The movie was directed by Girish Manukant and is also the first Gujarati cinema scope film. *'Kanku'*, a movie directed by Kantilal Rathod in the year 1969, based on the short story written by Pannalal Patel written in 1936, won the National Film Award for Best Feature Film in Gujarati at the 17th National Film Awards; also, the actress

Pallavi Mehta who played a lead in the movie won an award at the Chicago International Film Festival for her excellent performance in this movie. This movie was also the first movie from the industry to obtain widespread recognition worldwide.

Later, in the year 2008, a movie named *'The Better Half'* directed by Ashish Kakkad which targeted the urban audience in the industry, drew much attention of critics. This was also the first Gujarati film released from the industry on super 16 mm format. This movie also holds the record for the first movie from the industry to be released in multiplexes. In the year 2009, *'Little Zizou'* a movie directed by Sooni Taraporevala based on the screenplay of Sooni Taraporevala, won the Silver Lotus Award in the National Film Award for Best Film in the Family Welfare category at the 56th National Film Awards. Another movie which gained an international recognition was *'Veer Hamirji'* released in the year 2012, directed by Nilesh Indu Maruti Mohite based on the screenplay of Deven Shah. The movie was a historical film and was short-listed for Indian representation at the Oscars. The first Gujarati film selected from the industry to the Oscars was *'The Good Road,'* released in the year 2013, and directed by Gyan Correa. The film was also the Best Gujarati film at the 60th National Film Awards and was later awarded the Best Feature Film Jury Award at the Indian Film Festival held at Houston in the United States.

2.2.11 Odia Film Industry

The Odia film industry is a part of the Indian film industry, where motion pictures in Odia language are produced. It is the film industry based in Orissa and is popularly known as Ollywood. Mohan Sundar Deb Goswamiis considered as the pioneer of Odia cinema for bringing out the first full length motion picture on the Odia silver screen,*'Seeta Bibaha'* in the year 1936. He also performed the role of a producer for this movie which is also considered as the first complete Oriya film. The film was a huge commercial success and it paved the way for more such films in the Odia language. The film made with a budget of 30,000 rupees, consisted of 14 songs which were also a great hit. This film is also a great landmark film of the Oriya film Industry. Another movie named *'Roles to Eight'* directed by Kalyan Gupta and produced by RatikandaPandhi based on the screenplay of Kalicharan Pattanayak, Brundaban Mohapatra, and Kalyan Gupta. This film, released in the year 1951, was the first Oriya film with an English name. The movie was released almost 15 years after the release of first Oriya film, *'Sita Bibaha'*.

A major movie which excelled at the national levels was the *'Sri Lokenath'*, directed by PrafullaSengupta, which was released in the year 1960. The film was directed by Prafulla Sengupta, it also bagged a National Award in the year 1960. In the same year, itself, an actor from the industry Prasanta Nanda, received the National Award for the best actor as well. Later in the years 1960, 1966 and 1969, he won National Awards three times for his acting in the movies *'NuaBou'*, *'MatirManisha'* and *'Adina Megha'*. Another catalyst that helped the growth of the industry was the establishment of the Odisha Film Development Corporation in Cuttack in the year 1976. Later, films from the industry in 1985 and 2000 also scored two national awards for *'Hakim Babu'* directed by Pranab Das and Susanta Misra and by Biswaprakash respectively. Another major national recognition received for the industry was the National Film Award for the Best Supporting Actress received by ManjulaKanwar for her performance in the movie *'Bhanga Silata'*, released in the year 1987, and the National Film Award for the Best Child Artist was received by Tarasankar Misra for the performance in the movie *'Lavanya Preethi'*, which was released in the year 1994.

2.2.12 *Rajasthani Film Industry*

The Rajasthani film industry is a part of the Indian film industry, where motion pictures in Rajasthani language are produced. It is the film industry based in Rajasthan. A major landmark in the industry was the release of the movie *Nazrana,* which was released in the year 1942. This was the pioneer film produced in the industry. Another milestone happened only after nineteen years from the release of the '*Nazrana*' movie. A movie named '*BabasaRiLadli*', directed by B.K. Adarsh was released in the year 1961, which was the first Rajasthani movie with songs and filmed in colour. This movie was also the first blockbuster in the industry. Another notable movie released in the industry '*Bhawari*' which holds the record for the first Rajasthani film released in the industry through UFO Format. Between 1987 and 1995, a large number of films were produced in the industry, but only one single movie performed well in the theatres. It was '*Bai Chali Sasariye*' which was released in the year 1988. The movie was directed by Mohan Singh Rathod and was produced by Bharat Nahta. The music for this movie was given by OP Vyas. The songs in this movie also got much acceptance among the audience. Only around eighty movies were produced in the industry till date. In order to boost the film industry certain tax holidays were also announced by the government for the releases made in certain towns and cities; also, the government lowered the entertainment tax in the industry as well.

2.2.13 *Haryana Film Industry*

The Haryana film industry is a part of the Indian film industry,where motion pictures in Haryanvi language are produced, and is popularly known as Hariwood. The first film made in the industry was '*Harfull Singh Jaat Julani*', which was released in the year 1970. The film was directed by Anand Kumar. But the film could not perform well at the box office. Later in the year 1982, a movie named *'Bahuran'* was released. It was directed by, Arvind Swami, and distributed by Manmohan Bansal and was the first commercially successful movie in the industry. Later, in the year 1984,

'Chandrawal', a movie, directed by Devi Shankar Prabhakar was released. It was considered as the first commercially successful Haryanvi super hit movie. Another landmark movie in the industry was *'Laado'*, directed by Ashwini Chaudhary, and released in the year 2000. The movie won the Indira Gandhi Award for the Best First Film of a Director at the National Film Awards. This was also the first movie from the industry to win a national award. Till date, only 32 films were produced from the industry.

Another national recognition received for the industry was through the release of *'Pagdi'* the Honour movie. The screenplay as well direction for the movie was done by Rajeev Bhatia and the film was released in the year 2014. The film won two National Film Awards at the 62nd National Film Awards. One was for the Best Feature Film in Haryanvi and another was for the Best Supporting Actress, bagged by BaljinderKaur for her excellent performance in the movie.

2.2.14 Jammu and Kashmir Film Industry

The Jammu and Kashmir film industry is a part of the Indian film industry where motion pictures in Kashmiri language are produced. The first Kashmiri feature film in the industry was, *'Mainz Raat'*, which was released in the year 1964. The movie was directed by Jagiram Pal and was produced by MR Seth. This movie also bagged the President's Silver medal for excellence in the creation. The movie was a great inspiration to the later movies produced in the industry. Another major landmark in the industry was the release of *'Akh Daleel Loolech'*, which was directed by Aarshad Mushtaq. This was the first Kashmiri language digital feature film, which was premiered in India in 2006. The movie depicted the social and political struggles of the Kashmiri people during the 19th century. The film got much appreciation at the national levels, too. In the year 2012, another Kashmiri movie named *'Partav'* appeared as another landmark film in the industry. The film holds the record for the first 35mm feature film in the industry, it also bagged various international as well as national recognitions including the Award of Excellence from Canada International Film Festival held in the year 2013, Official selection for Kolkata International Film Festival 2013, Delhi International Film Festival 2013, Bengaluru International Film Festival 2013 and Third Eye Asian Film Festival 2014.

Another golden feather on the cap of Kashmiri film industry was the screening of the movie *'Pamposh'*, directed byEzra Mirunder. The screenplay was by Sanjit Narwekar. This was also the first movie from the industry to be screened at the Cannes Film Festival. In the year 2014, *Identity Card Ek Lifeline,* a movie directed and written by the Kashmiri filmmaker Rahat Kazmi received three awards at the American International Film Festival. It was a breakthrough for the industry worldwide. *'Valley of Saints'*, a movie which highlighted the environmental issues faced by the Dal Lake, was another major movie which was appreciated world-wide. The movie, directed by Musa Syeed and produced by Nicholas Bruckman, also won the World Dramatic Audience Award at Sundance Film Festival in the year 2012. There were many obstacles faced by the industry, such as lack of financial support from the government, problems relating to the cost-effective distribution channels, etc. Even though the government is providing various tax shelters and subsidy for entertainment tax, the industry is finding it hard to compete with the films produced around the globe.

3

Malayalam Cinema

Malayalam Cinema commonly known as Mollywood, is the based on the production of movie pictures in the Malayalam language. It is one of the majorIndian film ndustries based in the southern state of Kerala. The industry is the fourth biggest film industry in India in terms of movies released each year. Over the past decades, the Malayalam cinema has won immense demand all over India as well as abroad. The Malayalam cinema nowadays is performing much in foreign countries such as the United States, Australia, Germany, the UK and the Persian Gulf. Even though only a limited number of Malayalam cinemas is released overseas, those released abroad show excellence in collection and audience response.Generally, the history of Malayalam cinema can be divided into various eras in accordance with the technology used, the cast, the story used etc.

3.3.1 1907-1950s (1907-1950)

The first Malayalam cinema had to wait for a very long time after the exhibition of the first world cinema. The first Malayalam cinema was '*Vigathakumaran*' (The Lost Child), produced in 1928. The film was a silent movie, written, produced and directed by J.C Daniel, known as the "Father of Malayalam Cinema". The script work, direction, and camera handling for the film '*Vigathakumaran*' were done by JC Daniel himself. The theme selected for *'Vigathakumaran'*was of social significance. "The Travancore National Pictures" established by Daniel was the first film studio in Kerala. The film *'Vigathakumaran'* was an utter failure in the box office. Daniel suffered a lot inorder to overcome the situation and later sold his equipment and later closed his studio. However, Daniel made one more film, a martial arts documentary, *'Adithadi Murai'*. That film was also a complete failure and Daniel became bankrupt after the completion of this film. In 1907, the first movie hall in Kerala was established with a manually operated film projector, in Thrissur. The first permanent theatre in Kerala was established in Ollur, Thrissur, in the year 1913. After Daniel's death in 1975, the Kerala Government instituted the J. C. Daniel Award as a part of the Kerala State Film Awards, to honour lifetime achievements won by him to the Malayalam cinema. Later, the second Malayalam cinema *'Marthanda Varma'* (1933), directed by P.V. Rao and produced by R. Sundar Raj under the banner of Shri Rajeshwari Films, was released. The film was a historical silent film, based on the novel written by C.V. Raman Pillai, but it faced various legal problems and was reported a big failure in the box-office. The film was released only after five years from the release of the first Malayalam movie,Vigathakumaran. The film formed the base for the first copyright case in the history of Indian film industry. The third Malayalam cinema was *'Balan'* (1938) directed by S. Nottani and produced by R. Sundaram under the banner of Modern Theatres, Salem. K KAroor, Master Madanagopal, M V Shanku, K Gopinath, Alleppey Vincent, C.O.N Nambiar, M.K Kamalam, K.N Lakshmi andBaby Malathi formed the leading cast for this movie. The film was based on a social theme and was the first Malayalam film with sound in Malayalam. There were 24 songs in this film; the tunes were taken from popular Hindi and Tamil film tunes of that time; the film was a huge hit as well. The film was the first talkie in

Malayalam and it depicts the story of two orphaned children oppressed by their stepmother. During that period Malayalam films were produced at Chennai. Until 1947 Malayalam films continued to be produced by Tamil producers.

The later Malayalam films, up-to the end of the 1950s include *'Gnanambika'*(1940), *'Prahlada'*(1941), *'Nirmala'* (1941), *'Vellinakshatram'* (1949), *'Nalla Thanka'* (1950), *'Sthree'* (1950), *'Sasidharan'* (1950), *'Prasanna'* (1950), *'Chandrika'* (1950) and *'Chechi'* (1950).

The first cinema hall in Kerala was set up by K.V. Joseph in 1907. Later, in 1913, film projector which can be operated electronically was also set up by Jose Kattukaran. After that, several theatres were set up in various prominent cities in Kerala. One of the major milestones in the industry was the release of *'Nirmala'* in 1948, which introduced playback singing in Malayalam cinema. The first Malayali producer was P. J. Cherian, who produced *'Nirmala,* along with Joseph Cherian. The cinema *'Nirmala'* was based on a social theme, and was a big success. The first Malayalam movie shooting to be made in Kerala was that *'Vellinakshatram'* (1949) and it took shape at the Udaya Studios at Alleppey, set up in 1947. With the establishment of film studios in Kerala, there was a gradual shift of locations from Madras to Kerala. As a producer and director, Kunchacko made significant contributions to Malayalam cinema. He started Udaya Studios in Alleppey, in 1947, which boosted Malayalam film production in Kerala.

3.3.2 1950s (1951-1959)

With the beginning of the 1950s, various social issues formed the story base for Malayalam cinema. One such prominent film was *'Jeevitha Nouka'*, which was produced in 1950 and it depicted the problems in a joint family. The movie was a musical drama which tells about the problems in a joint family. This movie was much accepted bythe audience and was probably considered as the first "super hit" of Malayalam cinema. During this period, actor Sathyan emerged as a superstar in the industry. The movie *'Neelakkuyil'*, starring Sathyan and Premain, which was released in 1954, won the President's Silver Medel.The film showed excellence in scripting, acting, music and direction. The story for this movie was written by the veteran Malayalali novelist Uroob, and was directed jointly by P.Bhaskaran and Ramu Kariat. This film is considered as the first mature and authentic cinema in Malayalam film industry. The film was a huge success in the theatres as well.

Around 59 films were produced during that period, including *'Marumakal'*, *'Kanjana'*, *'Alphonsa'*, *'Velakaran'*, *'Thiramala'*, *'Avakashi'*, *'Sandeshi'*, *'CID'*, *'Aiyathi'*, *'Jayilpulli'*, *'Thaskaraveeran'* etc. In the initial years, the lyrics for movie songs were written in accordance with the tunes of Hindi and Tamil. During the end of the 1950s the arrival of popular poets and music directors' in Malayalam film industry brought the film music section a fresh beginning. Some of the famous poets of that period include ONV Kurup, P.Bhaskaran and Vayalar Rama Varma. This period also witnessed the emergence of blessed music directors including V. Dakshinamoorthy, Devarajan, Baburaj and Raghavan.

3.3.3 1960s (1960-69)

Many of the films of the 1960s concentrated on nationalist and socialist projects, and stressed the issues mainly relating to caste and class exploitation. The fight against obscurantist beliefs as well as the degeneration of the feudal class, was mainly highlighted in the movie stories of that period. The Malayalam film industry was also concerned with the breakup of the joint-family system. Some of the renowned directors of that period, includingRamuKariat, director of the movie *'Neelakkuyil'*, directors P. Bhaskaran and A. Vincent, also reached a high position in the industry by directing various hit films. *'Odayil Ninnu'*, *'Chemmeen'* (1965), *'Murappennu'* (1965), *'Iruttinte Athmavu'* (1966) were some of the most appreciated films of that decade. During this period, *'Bhargavi Nilayam'* which was released in 1964 and directed by A Vincent,appraredas the first horror film in Malayalam. The screenplay for this movie was written by Vaikom Muhammad Basheer; is one of the biggest hit movies of all time in Malayalam. The songs of this movie also received wide acceptance of that time. Another great achievement in Malayalam cinema was the advent of colour films, with the movie,*'Kandam Bacha Kottu'* (1961), directed by T. R. Sundaram. During that decade, the Malayalam film industry also won the President's Gold Medal for the best film *'Chemmeen'*, directed by Ramu Kariat in 1965, based on the story of veteran writer Thakazhi Sivasankara Pillai. This was the first Malayalam as well as South Indian film to win the National Film Award for the Best Feature Film. During the year 1969, the Kerala government started awarding "Kerala State Film Awards" for the films in Malayalam. The award was given to promote Malayalam films and to encourage artists, technicians and producers.

The story bases for the films of the 1960s were mainly nationalistic. The films of that decade concentrated mainly on issues relating to caste, class exploitation, degeneration of the feudal class, and also the breakup of the joint-family system. *'Chitramela'* movie, which was released in 1967, is considered as the first anthology film in the industry. The renowned actors of that period include Thikkurusi, Prem Nazir, Sathyan, Madhu, Adoor Bhasi, Bahadur, K.P.Ummer, Kottarakara Sreedharan Nair, Muthukulam, Joseprakash, Paravur Bharatan, Govindankutty, K.R.Vijaya, Ragini, Sharada, Sheela, Ambika, Jayabharathi, Aranmula Ponnamma, Adoor Bhavani, etc.

3.3.4 1970s (1970-1979)

In the 1970s, Malayalam cinema witnessed an international recognition. The film directed by Adoor Gopalakrishnan, *'Swayamvaram'* which was released in 1972, brought the industry to the international film arena. M. T. Vasudevan Nair's first film, *'Nirmalyam'*, won the National Film Award for the Best Feature Film. Cinematographers who won the National Award for their work on Malayalam films in the 1970s include P. S. Nivas for *'Mohiniyattam'* (1977), and Shaji N. Karun for *'Thampu'* (1979). In 1973, M. T. Vasudevan Nair, who was by then recognized as an important author in Malayalam, directed his first film *'Nirmalyam'*, which won the National Film Award for the Best Feature Film

During the 1970s, commercial cinemas were gaining much importance. M.G Soman and Sukumaran were some of the lead actors during that period. Also, action star Jayan also made an entry into the industry during that period, He is considered as the first genuine commercial superstar of Malayalam cinema. Adoor Gopalakrishnan's *'Swayamvaram'* won the National Film Award for the Best Director in 1972. But, independent film production in south India happened only two years after the release of *'Swayamvaran'*, when director P. Aravindan made the movie *'Kanchana Sita'* in 1974. Until that time, film production in Malayalam had been done with the financial and technical support of technicians from northern India. Another major landmark during the period was the movie, *'Thacholi Ambu'* which was released in 1978. It was theFirst Cinemascope film in Malayalam.

During the 1970s, Malayalam film industry saw the emergence of various film directors including G. Aravindan, John Abraham, P. A. Backer, P. N.Menon, I.V.Sasi, P. G. Viswambharan, K. G. George, Bharathan and Padmarajan. These directors directed various super-hit films based on the various social themes and the political views of that period. Besides, the popularity of film music also grew drastically during this period. In the year 1971, Muhammad Kutty Ismail Paniparambil (popularly known as Mammootty), one of the superstars of Malayalam film, made a debut into the industry by acting in the movie *'Anubhavangal Paalichakal'*, directed by K. S. Sethumadhavan.

3.3.5 1980s (1980-1989)

In the beginning of the 1980sthe audience witnessed Adoor Gopalakrishnan's magic touch again, with his movie,*'Elippathayam'* in 1981. The film brought the Malayalam cinema to a much higher level and also won the British Film Institute Award. Another major trendsetter during the era was director I.VSasi, who has directed more than 131 films, in 34 years. The release of *'My Dear Kuttichathan'* in 1984, which is the first 3D film in India, directed by Jijo Punnoose, was another golden feather in the cap of Malayalam movie industry. This film also bagged the Best Child Artist Award at the national level during that year. In 1986, a Malayalam film named *'Amma Ariyan'*, was made with money collected from the public, and the film's direction, screenplay and story were contributed by John Abraham. This film was the first film in India of that kind. During 1980-1989,more than 90 movies were released in the industry, and most of them earned a place in the super hit list. Another major milestone in the industry was the movie *'Piravi'* directed by Shaji. N. Karun in 1989, which bagged the Camera d'Or ("Golden Camera") award at the Cannes Film Festival. The Camera d'Or award is given for the best first feature film at the Cannes Film Festival. This film also bagged the most number of international awards in the Malayalam film history. Most of the movies produced during the period were rich with humour. Directors like Sathyan Anthikkad, Priyadarshan and Siddique-Lal have given a concrete base for humour in the industry. The end of the 1980's is considered as the

"Golden Age of Malayalam Cinema". The industry during the period also witnessed the emergence of eminent scriptwriters like M. T. Vasudevan Nair, Lohithadas and Sreenivasan. In the year 1980, Mohanlal Viswanathan Nair (popularly known as Mohanlal), considered as one of the superstars of Malayalam film, made a debut into the industry by acting in the movie *'Manjil Virinja Pookkal'* directed by Fazil. During the end of this era, *'Mathilukal'*, directed by Adoor Gopalakrishnan in 1989, obtained the record for the exhibition of a Malayalam movie for the most number of times in International film festivals. The period between the late 1980s and the early 1990s was the Golden Age of Malayalam Cinema.

3.3.6 1990s (1990-1999)

Malayalam cinema in the 1990s obtained various awards of international repute. During this period, worldwide recognition was obtained by the industry. One of the notable achivements during the period was the release of *'Swaham'* in 1994. This was the first Malayalam film which had competed for Palme d'Or of Cannes Film Festival. The film *'Swaham'* was directed by the veteran director Shaji N Karun. Another golden feather for the Malayalam film industry during the period was the official nomination of a Malayalam cinema to the Oscar. The movie selected for the Oscar nomination was *'Guru'* directed by Rajiv Anchal in 1997. Around 88 films were released during the period, and three dubbed movies, *'Sabarimala Sri Ayyappan'*, *'Avasanathe Rathri'* and *'Geethanjali'* were released during the period. Another great achievement of the Malayalam cinema was the starting of International Film Festival of Kerala (IFFK) was started. The IFFK was organised by Kerala State Chalachitra Academy on behalf of the Department of Cultural Affairs of the Kerala State Government. Compared to the past decades, the number of movies produced increased drastically. Also, the various technologies adopted by the directors haverise to a new show experience to the audience. Around 71 movies were produced during the period including three Malayalam dubbed movies. The major content of the movies of the period was comedy. Many hit movies based on comedy were produced during the period, and a majority of them were a huge success as well. A major landmark in the industry was the release of *'God Father'*.The film got the longest theatrical run in the history of Malayalam cinema.

3.3.7 2000s (2000-2009)

During this decade, also comedy films were produced enormously, in Malayalam. Comedy formed the basis for most of the successful movies produced during the period. *'CID Moosa'*, *'Meeshamadavan'*, and *'Kunjikoonan'* directed by Johny Antony, Lal Jose and Sasi Sanker respectively, were some of the movies which excelled in the box office during the period in this category. Many movie sequels were also produced during the period and most of them were successes. Another landmark film in the history of Malayalam cinema was the release of *'Twenty 20'* movie, written by Siby K Thomas and Udayakrishna. This movie was directed byJoshy and was produced on behalf of the Association of Malayalam Movie Artists (AMMA) for the purpose of raising funds for financially disabled actors in the industry. Another notable achievement of the Malayalam industry during the period was the release of the movie *'Moonnamathoral'* starring Jayaram and Samvrutha Sunil in lead roles and directed by V.K Prakash. This was the first movie in Malayalam film industry to be distributed in a digital format. However, the film couldn't excel in the box office much.

3.3.8 2010s (2010-Present)

The Malayalam film industry witnessed a drastic change during this era, regarding the selection of themes selected for films, directors etc. The conventional themes used for the films changed and an enormous number of directors and actors made a debut into the industry. This massive change was pioneered by Rajesh Pillai by directing the movie, '*Traffic*'. The screenplay for this movie was given by Prakash Sanjay and Prakash Bobby. The film was a top success in the box office and was considered as a forerunner for the new generation Malayalam cinema. More than 30 directors made a debut into the industry during this era. The achievement of this era was that most of the films directed by the debut directors were a top success, which showed a new path for the Malayalam film industry. During this era, the industry witnessed enormous landmarks as well. Jeethu Josepn directed themovie Drishyam, starring Mohanlal and Meena in lead roles. It collected 50 crore from the box office. This was the first Malayalam movie to enter into the 50-crore club. Later, in 2016 again Mohanlal starred '*Pulimurugan*' movie, directed by Vysakh which collected 150-crore worldwide. This was also the first Malayalam movie which entered the 100-crore club in collection. The screenplay for this movie was given by Udayakrishna; also, this movie was the third highest grossing South Indian movie of 2016. In this movie Mohanlal acted the role of a hunter hunting a tiger. The film also holds the record for the largest ever release for an Indian movie with 630 shows in the opening day, surpassing the records of '*Kabali*' the Tamil movie with 425 shows on the opening day. '*Adaminte Makan Abu*' was another notable film of that era. This film was chosen for the Best Foreign Film Category Award in 2011. A movie named '*Veeram*', released in 2016 and directed by Jayaraj, was produced at a cost of 35 crore. This movie holds the record for the most expensive movie produced in the Malayalam film industry till date.

3.4 Framework of Production and Maıketing Problems

The Film Producers, Distributors and Exhibitors functioning in the Malayalam film industry are facing enormous problems both in film production and in the marketing of films. The problems faced by them may differ on the basis of type of films produced, type of ownership in the production company, experience of film producers in the production field, concentration of producers in certain language films etc.The major production problems encountered by film producers functioning in Malayalam film industry include cast and crew related-problems, story, focus on stardom, copyright and intellectual property rights, difficulty in identification and obtaining of sources of fund and difficulty in obtaining of government grants on the other hand, the major marketing problems faced by them include piracy, tax, film certification problems, multiplexes, competition from other segments of the entertainment sector,etc.

The major marketing problems faced by exhibitors in the industry include Tax, Association, Multiplexes, Competition from Other Segments of Entertainment Sector and Difficulty in Obtaining Government Grants. Piracy, Ticket Prices, Sharing of Profits, Class of Theatre, Digital Revolution, E-Ticketing problems, Theatre Cess Percentage, Promotion Problems, Association and Tax,Competition from other Entertainment Sectors, Tax, Multiplex and Association are the vital issues faced by Cine Distributors in Malayalam Film industry.

3.5 Conclusion

From the theoretical background available, the film industry that we witness today is the result of various technological advancements and innovations put forward by eminent film makers in the industry. However, a complete solution for minimizing the problems in the industry is not formulated by the associations or by the government yet. Attempts to discover these problems and to minimize these problems are done on a large scale by experts.

REFERENCES

[1] Ababa Addis. (2016). For Ehiopians Mother India is Mother of All Bollywood Films, *The Hindu Sunday,* p.18.

[2] Abel Richard. (1996). *Silent Film,* TheAthlone Press, 194-198.

[3] Agnani Betty & Henry Aray. (2008). Subsidies and Awards in Movie Production, University of Granada.

[4] Ajith Kumar P.K. (2016). Mollywood Hails Court Order on Udta Punjab, *The Hindu,* p.2.

[5] Allam Richard. (1999). *Projecting Illusions, Films Spectatorships and Expressions of Reality,* Cambridge University Press Releases, 49-56.

[6] Anandan, S. (2016). Film Certification Board Plays Villain's Role, *The Hindu,* p. 2.

[7] JhaSomesh. (2016). Cinema Halls May Soon Work 24/7, *The Hindu,* p.16.

[8] Augustine Jose. (2006). *Flesher and Images,* pp. 55-61.

[9] Basu Anustup. (2010). *Bollywood in the Age of New Media,* Edinburgh University Press, 61-74.

[10] Belton John. (1996). Movies and Mass Culture, 40-43.

[11] BenegelShayam. (2006). A Door to Adoor, South Asian Cinema Foundation, 21-32.

[12] Bhowmik Someswar. (2009). *Cinema and Censorship the Politics of Control in India,* 1-6.

[13] Braun Edward. (1969). *Meyeshold on Theatre,* Melhurn and Company Limited, 76-79.

[14] Carney Raymond. (1986). *American Vision the Films of Prank Capra,* 271-275.

[15] ChakrabortySucheta. (2016). Everybody Loves Vincent, *The Hindu,* p.11.

[16] Cleve Bastian. (2006). *Film Production Management,* Focal Press Publication, 50-55.

[17] Cohen Keith. (1979). *Film and Fiction the Dynamic Exchange,* Yale University Press, 90-93.

[18] Cooper Darius. (2000).*The Cinema of Satyajit Ray Between Traditional and Modernity,* Cambridge University Press, 175-180.

[19] Dabashi Hamid. (2008). *The Making of a Rebel Filmmaker*, 63-79.

[20] Daftuar Swati. (2016). A Map with New Directions, *The Hindu Sunday Magazine,* p.9.

[21] Deleuze Gilles. (2005). *Deleuze Cinema,* 6-8.

[22] Densham D.H. (1959). *The Constitution of Research Films,* Pergamon Press, 4-16.

[23] Dix Andrew. (2011). *Beginning Film Studies,* 111-118.

[24] Dundoo Devi Sangeetha (2016). A Makeover in Progress, *The Hindu,* p.10.

[25] Easthope Antony. (1993). *Contemporary Film Theory,* 101-110.

[26] Egan Kelsey. (2014). Film Productions Design and Case Studies of the Great Gatsbby, *Elonn Journal of Undergraduate Researches in Communications,* Vol. 5, No. 1.

[27] Fielding Raymond. (1971).*The Technique of Special Effects Cinematography,* 15-23.

[28] Furstenaw Marc. (2010). The Film Theory Readers Debates and Arguments, 290 -293.

[29] Gabriel Karem. (2010). *Melodrama and the Nation, Sexual Economies of Bombay Cinema 1970-2000,* 69-88.

[30] Gera Anjali. (2012). *The Magic of Bollywood at Home and Abroad,* Sage Publications India Pvt Linited, 69-78.

[31] Gokulsing Moti &Dissanayake Wimal. (2000). *Indian Popular Cinema- A Narrative of Cultural Change,* Orient Longman Publication, 56-94.

[32] Gokulsing Moti, & Dissanayake Wimal.(1988). *Indian Popular Cinema- A Narrative of Cultural Change,* Baba Barkha Nath Press, New Delhi, 117-120.

[33] Gopinath Swapna. & Raj Jalarajan Sony. (2015). Gender Construct as a Narrative and Text: The Female Protagonist in New Generation Malayalam Cinema, South Asian Popular Culture.

[34] Harbord Janet. (2002). *Film Cultures,* Sage Publication, 48-52.

[35] Hood John. (2009). *The Essential Mystery Major Filmmakers of Indian art Cinema,* 9-15.

[36] Ibkar Alisha. (2015). The Natyasastras and Indian Cinemas: A Study of Rasa Theory as a Cornerstone for Indian Aesthetics, *International Journal of English Languages & Translation Studies,* 80-87.

[37] Indraganti Krishna Mohana. (2016). Faith in the Formula Film, *The Hindu,* p.9.

[38] Joshi Namrata. (2016). Canvases on Celluloid, *The Hindu,* p.11.

[39] Joshi Namrata. (2016). Letting Our Films Fly, *The Hindu* Daily, p.9.

[40] Joshi Namrata. (2016). Nothing Queer about Gay Films, *The Hindu Daily,* p.13.

[41] K Bhumika. (2016). Predominant Voice in Cinema Still that of Men, *The Hindu,* p.9.

[42] Kaur Raminder& Sinha Ajay. (2000). *Bollywood Popular Indian Cinema through a Transnational Lens,* Sage Publication, New Delhi, 14-18.

[43] Kavoori Anandan,& PunathambekarAswin.(2009). *Global Bollywood,* Oxford University Press, 7-10.

[44] Kazmi Fareed. (1999). *The Politics of India's Conventional Cinema,* Sage Publication, New Delhi, 79-87.

[45] KhajaneMuralidhara. (2016). Censor Board is Often Misused by Party in Power, *The Hindu,* p.9.

[46] Khan Zara. (2016). Netflix So What, *The Hindu Sunday Magazine,* p.1.

[47] Kidiyoor Gururaj, Yatgiri Prashant & Shetty Ranjan Sham. (2015). *Kannada Film Industry Challenges and the Way Forward,* Karnataka Chalanchitra Academy.

[48] Kumar Krishna, Kumar Ajith. (2016). Monsoon Surprise at Box Office, *The Hindu Sunday Edition,* p.2.

[49] Kumar Naresh. (1995). *Indian Cinema Ebbs and Tides,* Har-Anand Publication, New Delhi, 17-23.

[50] Kumar Rajinder. (2006). *Sociology Goes to the Movies,* Sage Publications, 15-31.

[51] Labato Ramon. (2012). Shadow Publications, 11-15.

[52] Lent John. (1990). *The Asian Film Industry,* Christopher Helm Publishing Company, 55-59.

[53] Mamer Bruce. (2000). *Film Production Technique Creating the Accomplished Image,* 16-31.

[54] Mathur Meera; & Goswami Shubham. (2012). A Study of Consumers Behavior and Product Palacement in Indian Cinema, *Annals of Management Research,* Volume 2, No 1.

[55] Mazumdar Ranjani. (2007). *Bombay Cinema an Archive of the City,* 45-52.

[56] Mohan Jag. (1984). *S. Sukhdev Film Maker- A Documentary Montage,* 99-116.

[57] Mohan Jag. (1990). *Documentary Film and Indian Awakening,* Publication Division, 35-37.

[58] Mukherjee Akaitab. (2014). Theory of Indian Cinema, *International Journal of English, Language, Journal and Humanities,* Volume II, Issue VII, November 2014.

[59] Mulvey Laura. (1975). *Visual Pleasure and Narrative Cinema,* Film Psychology, Society and Ideology.

[60] Nagarajan Saraswathy. (2016). Lights Camera Action, Friday Review Arts and Culture, *The Hindu,* p.1.

[61] Nath Divesh. (2016). Art of Visual Storytelling. Education Plus, *The Hindu Sunday,* p.4.

[62] Nazeer Mohamed. (2015). An Unsound Trend in Mollywood, *The Hindu Daily,* p.13.

[63] NeuTimm. (2007).Bollywood is coming Copyright and Film Industry Issues Regarding International Film Co-Productions Involving India, Cornell Law School Graduate Student Papers.

[64] Nicholas Bill. (2010). *Engaging Cinema an Introduction to Film Studies,* 150-156.

[65] Noonan Keith. (2016). 3 Trends That Will Shape the Movie Industry in 2016, *The Motley Fool,* 11-16.

[66] Oommen, M.A, Joseph, K.V. (1990). *Economics of Indian Cinema,* C-DIT Series, 14-19.

[67] Ouyang Chun, HofstedeTer Arthur, Rosa La Marcello, Rosemann Michael. (2008). *Camera, Set, Action Automating Film Production via Business Process Management,* p.1.

[68] Parayil Kumar Sujith. (2014). *Synoptique —An Online Journal of Film and Moving Images Studies.*

[69] Park James. (1984). *Learning to Dream the New British Cinema,* Faber and Faber Publishers, London, 53-61.

[70] Praveen, M.P. (2016). When Mollywood Trailers Steal the Show, *The Hindu,* p.2.

[71] Rabiger Michael. (2004). *Directing the Documentary,* Panchsheel Garden, 23-68.

[72] Rajadhyaksha Ashish. (2009). I*ndian Cinema in Time of Celluloid from Bollywood to the Emergency,* 10-13.

[73] Ramachandran Naman. (2016). We Get High on Cinema, *The Hindu Sunday Magazine,* p.1.

[74] Raman Giji. (2016). Giving a Kung Fu Punch to Films, *The Hindu,* p.2.

[75] RanganBaradwaj. (2016). Back to Blaming the Movies, *The Hindu,* p.9.

[76] RanganBaradwaj. (2016). Moving Images Moving Words. *The Hindu Sunday Magazine,* p.3.

[77] Rangan Baradwaj. (2016). Small Film – Metaphysical Weight, *The Hindu Sunday Magazine,* p.3.

[78] Rangan Baradwaj. (2016).If Rushes were Horses, Screening Room, *The Hindu,* p.3.

[79] Rao Mohit. (2016). Romas go to Bollywood, *The Hindu Sunday Magazine,* p.2.

[80] Ray Satyajit. (1976). *Our Films Their Films,* Oxford Printing Press, 21-72.

[81] Robinson, M.N. (1939). *The Film Answers Book,* Great Britain Press, 45-48.

[82] Rothman William. (2004). *The I of the Camera,* 2-10.

[83] Sarkar Kabita. (1975). I*ndian Cinema Today an Analysis,* Sterling Publishers Private Limited, 110-116.

[84] Sen Aditi. (2016). Putting up a Good Fight, The Hindu, p.11.

[85] Sexena Ambrish. (2004). *Indian Cinema Society and Culture,* Kanishka Publishers, New Delhi, 16-19.

[86] Shahani Parmesh. (2015). Mumbai the Ultimate Jugaad City, *The Hindu Newspaper,* p.16.

[87] Shingler Martin. (2012). *Star Studio a Critical Guide,* Palgrave Macmillian Publication, 40-47.

[88] Srinivas S.V. (2009). *Megastar Chiranjeevi and Telugu Cinema after NT Rama Rao,* Oxford University Press, New Delhi, 16-23.

[89] Stapes Donald. (1973). *The American Cinema,* New York University, 1-8.

[90] Steven Peter. (1985). *Jump Cut Hollywood Politics and Counter Cinema,* 63-68.

[91] Stishova Yelena. (1989). *Look Who's here: A New Trend in the Soviet Cinemas,* Panchsheel Publishers, 22-46.

[92] Swann Pau. (1987). *The Hollywood Films in Post War Britain,* CroomHelm Publications, 61-64.

[93] Turner Graeme. (1988). *Film as Social Practice,* Routledge Press, 29-38.

[94] Turner Graeme. (1999). *Film as a Social Practice,* Routledge Taylor and Francis Group, 47-50.

[95] Turok Ivan. (2003). Cities, Clusters and Creative Industry: A Case of Films and Televisions in Scotland, *European Planning Studies,* Vol. 11, No. 5.

[96] Vasudev Aruna. (1978). *Liberty and Licence in the Indian Cinema,* Vikas Publications, 2-10.

[97] Vasudevan Rani. (2010). *The Melodramatic Public Film Forms and Spectatorship in Indian Cinema,* Permanent Black Publication, 16-31.

[98] Vitali Valentina, & Willemen Paul. (2006). *Theorising National Cinema,* PalgraveMacmillian Publication, 17-26.

[99] Wagner Robert. (1975). The Education of the Film Maker an International View, The UNESCO Press, 30-34.

[100] Walter Ernest. (1969). *Film Cutting Room,* Focal Press, London, 16-31.

[101] Watkins Beth. (2016). Two Moods of Bengali Cinema, *The Hindu,* p.11.

[102] Woods Jeanie. (2011). *Vision of Empires and others Imagining Cinemas of Ireland and India, 1910-1962,* 28-36.

4

Production and Marketing Problems of Film Producers in Kerala

The film producers functioning in the Malayalam film industry are facing enormous problems both in film production and in the marketing of films. The problems faced by them may differ on the basis of the type of films produced, type of ownership in the production company, experience of film producers in the production field, concentration of producers in certain language films, etc. The major production and marketing problems encountered by them include increased tax rates, difficulty in the obtainment of various grants from the government, disputes that are arising between various producers' associations prevailing in the industry, etc. Also the various charges and fees imposed by government authorities from time to time, difficulty in the obtainment of institutional funds from banks and other financial institutions for expanding their production and marketing channel, and various costs and huge delay incurred in film certification process, etc, are other major problems encountered.

Here, inorder to study in detail the production and marketing problems faced by film producers in the Malayalam film industry, a sample of 80 producers was selected from a total population of 113, using simple random sampling method. Out of the sample of 80 only 30 film producers are focused in the production of Malayalam movies, and 50 film producers are focused in the production and distribution of Malayalam films. When considering the experience of the selected producers in film production, 46.3 per cent of them have more than 20 years of experience in film production, followed by producers having an experience ranging from 16-20 years.

A structured questionnaire was designed and data collected from these 80 respondents. Various problem areas of production and distribution such as Tax, Story, Difficulty in the Obtainment of Government Grants, Competition from Other Segments of Entertainment Sectors, Piracy, Film Certification Problems, etc, have beentaken into account inorder to study the production and marketing problems faced by the film producers in Malayalam movie industry.

Statistical techniques such as F Test, Canonical Discriminant Analysis, etc., have also been used in-order to understand in detail the relation between these problems.

4.1 Frequency Distribution of the Producers Selected for the Study

The following Tables 4.1, 4.2, 4.3 and 4.4 show the selected film producers' ownership in the production company, their movie production concentration, movie operation and experience in production.

Table 4.1 Type of Ownership in the Company

	Frequency	*Percentage*	*Valid Percentage*	*Cumulative Percentage*
Single	44	55.0	55.0	55.0
Partnership	36	45.0	45.0	100.0
Total	80	100.0	100.0	

(Source: Primary data)

Table 4.2 Concentration in Movie Production

	Frequency	*Percentage*	*Valid Percentage*	*Cumulative Percentage*
Malayalam	80	100.0	100.0	100.0

(Source: Primary data)

Table 4.3 Producer's Operation

	Frequency	*Percentage*	*Valid Percentage*	*Cumulative Percentage*
Production Only	30	37.5	37.5	37.5
Production and Distribution	50	62.5	62.5	100.0
Total	80	100.0	100.0	

(Source: Primary data)

Table 4.4 Experience in Movie Production

	Frequency	*Percentage*	*Valid Percentage*	*Cumulative Percentage*
11-15 Years	7	8.8	8.8	8.8
16-20 Years	36	45.0	45.0	53.8
Above 20 Years	37	46.3	46.3	100.0
Total	80	100.0	100.0	

(Source: Primary data)

From the Table 4.1, it is clear that 55 per cent of the selected film producers have a single form of ownership in the company and 45 per cent had a partnership form of ownership. So, it can be concluded that a majority of the cine producers have a single form of ownership in the company. While analyzing Table 4.2, it is observed that 100 per cent of the selected producers functioning in the industry in Kerala are concentrating in Malayalam films.

This means that the majority of the films produced in the industry in Kerala are in Malayalam. From Table 4.3, it is evident that 62.5 per cent of the selected producers functioning in the industry are operating in production and distribution of movies followed by producer's operating in production alone. So, it is evident that the majority of the film producers operating in the industry were concentrating more in production and distribution of films. From Table 4.4, it can be concluded that 46.3 per cent of the selected film producers functioning in the industry have an experience above 20 years, followed by producers having 16-20 years experience and 11-15 years experience. So, we can conclude that the majority of the film producers functioning in the industry have above 20 years of experience.

4.2 Production Problems of Film Producers

One of the major problems encountered by producers in the industry is difficulty in the obtaining of government grants for production of movies. The lack of financial support from the State and Central Governments in obtaining grants for movie production is a major hindrance to film producers functioning in the industry. Also huge delays incurred in the sanctioning of grants, and distribution of grants, only for certain types of films produced in the industry, are also a major problem affecting the industry. The presence of strict procedures in obtaining grants from the government and difference in laws between Central and State Governments in providing grants to producers are also other hindrances in the obtaining of these grants. The following Table shows the mean scores of the responses of selected Film Producers towards the Difficulty in Obtaining Government Grants.

Table 4.5 Tests of Between-Subjects Effects

Dependent Variable : Government Grant					
Source	*Type I Sum of Squares*	*Df*	*Mean Square*	*F*	*Sig.*
Type of Ownership in the Company	14651.008	1	14651.008	151.950	***.000****
Producer's Operation	7.170	1	7.170	.074	.786
Experience in Production	2700.542	2	1350.271	14.004	***.000****
Error	7231.480	75	96.420		
Total	24590.200	79			

*Significant at 5 per cent level

(Source: Primary data)

4.2.1 Estimated Marginal Means

Table 4.6 Type of Ownership in the Company

Dependent Variable: Government Grant				
Type of Ownership in the Company	*Mean*	*Std. Error*	*95% Confidence Interval*	
			Lower Bound	*Upper Bound*
Single	34.975	1.653	31.681	38.269
Partnership	**69.279**	3.989	61.333	77.226

(Source: Primary data)

Table 4.7 Producer's Operation

Dependent Variable: Government Grant				
Producer's Operation	*Mean*	*Std. Error*	*95% Confidence Interval*	
			Lower Bound	*Upper Bound*
Production Only	**53.934**	4.208	45.551	62.318
Production and Distribution	50.320	1.648	47.037	53.603

(Source: Primary data)

Table 4.8 Experience in Production

Dependent Variable: Government Grant				
Experience in Production	*Mean*	*Std. Error*	*95% Confidence Interval*	
			Lower Bound	*Upper Bound*
11-15 Years	**63.959**	5.598	52.808	75.111
16-20 Years	41.959	1.946	38.084	45.835
Above 20 Years	50.462	1.646	47.184	53.740

(Source: Primary data)

As per the Tables 4.5, 4.6, 4.7, and 4.8, it may be understood that the Difficulty in the Obtaining of Government Grants is very high for film producers having a partnership type of ownership in the company (Mean 69.279), and that producers who concentrate on production only face this problem very seriously (Mean 53.934). At the same time, considering the experience in production, the producers having an experience of 11-15 yearsface this problem more seriously than other categories of producers. The mean score variation is found significant at 5 per cent level (P<.05) for type of ownership in the production company and experience of producers in production, but not significant to producers movie operation.

4.2.2 *Cast and Crew*

Another major problem encountered by producers in the industry is the identification and hiring of the perfect cast and crew for the movie. Film crew is a group of persons hired by a production company,that is, experts who have a specialized skill in specific aspects of film production, such as direction, camera handling, stunt performance, production coordination, film editing, etc. On the other hand, film casting refers to choosing a particular actor, singer, dancer etc for performing a role mentioned in the movie script. The selection is made in consultation with the director and screenplay writer. Difficulty in choosing the perfect man both as cast and as crew, is a major problem faced by the film producers.The following Table shows the mean scores of the responses of selected Film Producers towards the identification and hiring of Cast and Crew.

Table 4.9 Tests of Between-Subjects Effects

Dependent Variable: Cast and Crew

Source	*Type I Sum of Squares*	*Df*	*Mean Square*	*F*	*Sig.*
Type of Ownership in the Company	4359.517	1	4359.517	99.779	***.000****
Producer's Operation	213.861	1	213.861	4.895	***.030****
Experience in Production	325.527	2	162.763	3.725	***.029****
Error	3276.896	75	43.692		
Total	8175.800	79			

**Significant at 5 per cent level*

(Source: Primary data)

Estimated Marginal Means

Table 4.10 Type of Ownership in the Company

Dependent Variable : Cast and Crew				
Type of Ownership in the Company	*Mean*	*Std. Error*	*95% Confidence Interval*	
			Lower Bound	*Upper Bound*
Single	17.970	1.113	15.753	20.187
Partnership	**34.757**	2.685	29.408	40.106

(Source: Primary data)

Table 4.11 Producer's Operation

Dependent Variable : Cast and Crew				
Producer's Operation	*Mean*	*Std. Error*	*95% Confidence Interval*	
			Lower Bound	*Upper Bound*
Production Only	**26.913**	2.833	21.270	32.556
Production and Distribution	25.814	1.109	23.604	28.024

(Source: Primary data)

Table 4.12 Experience in Production

Dependent Variable: Cast and Crew				
Experience in Production	*Mean*	*Std. Error*	*95% Confidence Interval*	
			Lower Bound	*Upper Bound*
11-15 Years	**32.943**	3.768	25.436	40.449
16-20 Years	23.943	1.310	21.334	26.552
Above 20 Years	22.205	1.108	19.999	24.412

(Source: Primary data)

As per Tables 4.9, 4.10, 4.11, and 4.12, it can be observed that the problem of cast and crew is very high for producers having a partnership type of ownership in the company (Mean 34.757) and producers who concentrate on production only face this problem more seriously (Mean 26.913). At the same time considering the experience in production, the producers having an experience of 11 – 15 years face this problem more seriously than other categories of producers. The mean score variation is found significant at 5 per cent level (P<.05) for all categories of film producers functioning in the industry.

4.2.3 Focus on Stardom

Yet another major hindrance faced by producers in the industry is the focus on film stars rather than on the story and script. Many a time, the screenplay for the movie is edited in accordance with the vested interests of the film actors. So, what the screenplay writer thinks and imagines in mind is not pictured in the actual film. Often, these types of editions made by the actors leads to certain conflicts at the time of shooting films. Also, the presence of various associations in the industry sometimes makes the situation more complicated. The following Table shows the mean scores of the responses of selected Film Producers towards the identification and hiring of Cast and Crew.

Table 4.13 Tests of Between-Subjects Effects

Dependent Variable : Focus on Stardom

Source	*Type I Sum of Squares*	*Df*	*Mean Square*	*F*	*Sig.*
Type of Ownership in the Company	761.608	1	761.608	19.605	***.000****
Producer's Operation	4222.920	1	4222.920	108.702	***.000****

Experience in Production	4907.640	2	2453.820	63.164	*.000**
Error	2913.632	75	38.848		
Total	12805.800	79			

*Significant at 5 per cent level

(Source: Primary data)

Estimated Marginal Means

Table 4.14 Type of Ownership in the Company

Dependent Variable : Focus on Stardom				
Type of Ownership in the Company	*Mean*	*Std. Error*	*95% Confidence Interval*	
			Lower Bound	*Upper Bound*
Single	36.922	1.050	34.831	39.013
Partnership	**46.160**	2.532	41.116	51.204

(Source: Primary data)

Table 4.15 Producer's Operation

Dependent Variable : Focus on Stardom				
Producer's Operation	*Mean*	*Std. Error*	*95% Confidence Interval*	
			Lower Bound	*Upper Bound*
Production Only	39.167	2.671	33.846	44.489
Production and Distribution	**43.915**	1.046	41.831	45.999

(Source: Primary data)

Table 4.16 Experience in Production

Dependent Variable : Focus on Stardom				
Experience in Production	*Mean*	*Std. Error*	*95% Confidence Interval*	
			Lower Bound	*Upper Bound*
11-15 Years	**65.245**	3.553	58.167	72.323
16-20 Years	28.245	1.235	25.785	30.705
Above 20 Years	31.133	1.044	29.053	33.214

(Source: Primary data)

Tables 4.13, 4.14, 4.15 and 4.16, show that the problem of focus on stardom was very high for film producers who had a partnership form of ownership in the production company (Mean score 46.160). At the same time, producers having an experience of 11-15 years faced the problem more seriously than other categories of producers in the industry. The mean score variation is found significant at 5 per cent level of significance for all categories of film producers functioning in the industry.

4.2.4 Copyright and Intellectual Property Rights

One of the major problems encountered by film producers in the industry is the prevalence of stringent rules and regulations in obtaining various Copyright and Intellectual Property Rights. Producers are mostly using these tools for protecting hit stories, music and characters' names from unauthorized access by making use of the tools that are prevailing in the industry. The high cost incurred in obtaining these copyrights, and frequent alterations which are made on these rules by changing government bodies, are also a major problem affecting producers in the industry. In addition to that, lack of knowledge on the part of producers in understanding the correct procedures for obtaining these rights lawfully makes the situation worse. The following Tables show the mean scores of the responses of selected Film Producers towards the problem of Copyright and Intellectual Property Rights.

Table 4.17 Tests of Between-Subjects Effects

Dependent Variable : Copyright and Intellectual Property Rights

Source	*Type I Sum of Squares*	*Df*	*Mean Square*	*F*	*Sig.*
Type of Ownership in the Company	2171.415	1	2171.415	46.168	***.000****
Producer's Operation	1483.533	1	1483.533	31.543	***.000****
Experience in Production	1297.993	2	648.997	13.799	***.000****
Error	3527.446	75	47.033		
Total	8480.388	79			

*Significant at 5 per cent level

(Source: Primary data)

Estimated Marginal Means

Table 4.18 Type of Ownership in the Company

Dependent Variable : Copyright and Intellectual Property Rights

Type of Ownership in the Company	*Mean*	*Std. Error*	*95% Confidence Interval*	
			Lower Bound	*Upper Bound*
Single	23.923	1.155	21.623	26.224
Partnership	**49.631**	2.786	44.081	55.181

(Source: Primary data)

Table 4.19 Producer's Operation

Dependent Variable : Copyright and Intellectual Property Rights

Producer's Operation	*Mean*	*Std. Error*	*95% Confidence Interval*	
			Lower Bound	*Upper Bound*
Production Only	**45.522**	2.939	39.667	51.377
Production and Distribution	28.033	1.151	25.740	30.326

(Source: Primary data)

Table 4.20 Experience in Production

Dependent Variable : Copyright and Intellectual Property Rights

Experience in Production	*Mean*	*Std. Error*	*95% Confidence Interval*	
			Lower Bound	*Upper Bound*
11-15 Years	**46.598**	3.909	38.810	54.387
16-20 Years	29.598	1.359	26.892	32.305
Above 20 Years	34.135	1.149	31.845	36.424

(Source: Primary data)

As per Tables 4.17, 4.18, 4.19, and 4.20, it is evident that the problem of Copyright and Intellectual Property Rights is found very high for producers having a partnership type of ownership in the company (Mean 46.631) and that producers who concentrate on production only face this problem very seriously (Mean 45.522). At the same time, considering the experience in production, the producers having an experience of 11 – 15 years face this problem more severely than other categories of producers. The mean score variation is found significant at 5 per cent level ($P<.05$) for all categories of film producers functioning in the industry.

4.2.5 Difficulty in the Identification and Obtaining of Sources of Funds

One of the major problems encountered by film producers in the industry is the Difficulty in the Identification and Obtaining of Sources of Funds from banks and other financial institutions. There is a great hesitation on the part of the bank authorities in providing funds for film production. Also, the producers find it very difficult for providing adequate assets as collateral security for loans which makes the delay longer. The presence of strict procedures in obtaining funds from banks and government agencies, and the lack of financial support from State and Central governments are also great problems faced by the film producers in the industry. The following Table shows the mean scores of the responses of selected Film Producers towards the Difficulty in the Identification and Obtaining of Sources of Funds.

Table 4.21 Tests of Between-Subjects Effects

Dependent Variable : Difficulty in Identification and Obtaining of Sources of Funds

Source	*Type I Sum of Squares*	*Df*	*Mean Square*	*F*	*Sig.*
Type of Ownership in the Company	5723.900	1	5723.900	107.622	***.000****
Producer's Operation	39.465	1	39.465	.742	.392
Experience in Production	1662.632	2	831.316	15.631	***.000****
Error	3988.890	75	53.185		
Total	11414.887	79			

*Significant at 5 per cent level

(Source: Primary data)

Estimated Marginal Means

Table 4.22 Type of Ownership in the Company

Dependent Variable : Difficulty in Identification and Obtaining of Sources of Fund

Type of Ownership in the Company	*Mean*	*Std. Error*	*95% Confidence Interval*	
			Lower Bound	*Upper Bound*
Single	23.209	1.228	20.762	25.655
Partnership	**48.201**	2.963	42.299	54.103

(Source: Primary data)

Table 4.23 Producer's Operation

Dependent Variable : Difficulty in Identification and Obtaining of Sources of Fund

Producer's Operation	*Mean*	*Std. Error*	*95% Confidence Interval*	
			Lower Bound	*Upper Bound*
Production only	**38.859**	3.125	32.633	45.086
Production and Distribution	32.550	1.224	30.112	34.989

(Source: Primary data)

Table 4.24 Experience in Production

Dependent Variable : Difficulty in Identification and Obtaining of Sources of Fund

Experience in Production	*Mean*	*Std. Error*	*95% Confidence Interval*	
			Lower Bound	*Upper Bound*
11-15 Years	**45.651**	4.157	37.369	53.933
16-20 Years	27.651	1.445	24.772	30.529
Above 20 Years	33.813	1.222	31.378	36.247

(Source: Primary data)

By analyzing Tables 4.21, 4.22, 4.23, and 4.24, it can be observed that the problem of Difficulty in Identification and Obtaining of Sources of Funds is very high for Producers having a partnership type of ownership in the company (Mean 48.201), and that producers who concentrate on production only face this problem more seriously (Mean 38.859). At the same time, considering the experience in production, producers having an experience of 11-15 years face this problem more seriously than other categories of producers. The mean score variation is found significant at 5 per cent level (P<.05) for type of ownership in the production company and experience of producer in production, but not significant for producer's movie operation.

4.2.6 Visual Effects Industry

A very serious problem faced by producers in the industry is the rapid growth of visual effects industry. Difficulty in the identification of skilled persons for making visual effects and less awareness on the part of producers about the immense technologies available in the market constitutes the major drawback for the growth of the industry. In addition to that, the huge remuneration charged by technicians and the difficulty in choosing the right persons for the job create a major hindrance faced by the film producers in the industry.The following Table shows the mean scores of the responses of selected Film Producers towards the Visual Effects Industry.

Table 4.25 Tests of Between-Subjects Effects

Dependent Variable : Visual Effects Industry

Source	*Type I Sum of Squares*	*Df*	*Mean Square*	*F*	*Sig.*
Type of Ownership in the Company	1920.455	1	1920.455	50.334	***.000****
Producer's Operation	2.079	1	2.079	.054	.816

Experience in Production	432.889	2	216.445	5.673	*.005**
Error	2861.577	75	38.154		
Total	5217.000	79			

*Significant at 5 per cent level

(Source: Primary data)

Estimated Marginal Means

Table 4.26 Type of Ownership in the Company

Dependent Variable : Visual Effects Industry

Type of Ownership in the Company	*Mean*	*Std. Error*	*95% Confidence Interval*	
			Lower Bound	*Upper Bound*
Single	15.609	1.040	13.537	17.681
Partnership	**30.956**	2.509	25.958	35.955

(Source: Primary data)

Table 4.27 Producer's Operation

Dependent Variable : Visual Effects Industry

Producer's Operation	*Mean*	*Std. Error*	*95% Confidence Interval*	
			Lower Bound	*Upper Bound*
Production Only	**25.951**	2.647	20.678	31.225
Production and Distribution	20.614	1.037	18.549	22.679

(Source: Primary data)

Table 4.28 Experience in Production

Dependent Variable : Visual Effects Industry				
Experience in Production	*Mean*	*Std. Error*	*95% Confidence Interval*	
			Lower Bound	*Upper Bound*
11-15 Years	**30.342**	3.521	23.328	37.357
16-20 Years	19.342	1.224	16.904	21.780
Above 20 Years	20.163	1.035	18.101	22.225

(Source: Primary data)

From Tables 4.25, 4.26, 4.27 and 4.28, it can be seen that the problem of visual effects industry is found very high for Producers having a partnership type of ownership in the company (Mean 30.956), and that producers who concentrate on production only face this problem the most (Mean 25.951). At the same time, considering the experience in production, producers having an experience of 11–15 years face this problem more seriously than other categories of producers. The mean score variation is found significant at 5 per cent level (P<.05) for type of ownership in the production company and experience of the producer in production, but not significant for producer's movie operation.

4.3 Marketing Problems of Film Producers

4.3.1 Piracy

One of the most vital marketing problems faced by film producers in the industry is piracy. The absence of strict rules and regulations on the part of Central Government as well as State Government hasmade piracy rampant in the industry. Lack of coordination between producers' and cine exhibitors' associations in curbing piracy is another major problem. Lack of knowledge on the part of producers in identifying and destroying the devices and sites used for uploading movies makesthe piracy issue more complicated. Various statistics show that there is a drastic demand for the pirated version movies in the society. The truth is that if everyone pirates the movies, then no creative work can get done in the industry. The most effective method to curtail this problem is to make the law very strong. The following Table shows the mean scores of the responses of Selected Film Producers towards the problem of Piracy.

Table 4.29 Tests of Between-Subjects Effects

Dependent Variable: Piracy

Source	*Type I Sum of Squares*	*Df*	*Mean Square*	*F*	*Sig.*
Type of Ownership in the Company	9675.823	1	9675.823	86.516	***.000****
Producer's Operation	570.861	1	570.861	5.104	***.027****
Experience in Production	882.954	2	441.477	3.947	***.023****
Error	8387.912	75	111.839		
Total	19517.550	79			

**Significant at 5 per cent level*

(Source: Primary data)

Estimated Marginal Means

Table 4.30 Type of Ownership in the Company

Dependent Variable : Piracy

Type of Ownership in the Company	*Mean*	*Std. Error*	*95% Confidence Interval*	
			Lower Bound	*Upper Bound*
Single	35.488	1.781	31.940	39.035
Partnership	**57.042**	4.296	48.484	65.600

(Source: Primary data)

Table 4.31 Producer's Operation

Dependent Variable : Piracy				
Producer's Operation	*Mean*	*Std. Error*	*95% Confidence Interval*	
			Lower Bound	*Upper Bound*
Production Only	43.894	4.532	34.866	52.923
Production and Distribution	**48.635**	1.775	45.099	52.171

(Source: Primary data)

Table 4.32 Experience in Production

Dependent Variable : Piracy				
Experience in Production	*Mean*	*Std. Error*	*95% Confidence Interval*	
			Lower Bound	*Upper Bound*
11-15 Years	**53.406**	6.029	41.397	65.416
16-20 Years	40.406	2.095	36.232	44.580
Above 20 Years	44.982	1.772	41.451	48.512

(Source: Primary data)

Tables 4.29, 4.30, 4.31 and 4.32 depict that the problem of piracy much affects film producers who have a partnership form of ownership in the production company (Mean 57.042). At the same time, considering the experience of film producers in production, the producers having an experience of 11-15 years face the problem more seriously than other categories of producers in the industry. Also, the producers operating in production and distribution face this problem the most. The mean score variation is found significant at 5 per cent level (P<.05) for all categories of film producers functioning in the industry.

4.3.2 Tax

Yet another dominant marketing problem encountered by film producers in the industry is that of taxes. The taxes are imposed by the Central Government, State Government and the local bodies like municipalities and panchayaths. The Government levies tax in the form of sales tax, entertainment tax, multiplex tax, service tax, CBFC tax, etc. The rates of tax levied by these Government bodies are also of great difference. Another most important problem regarding taxes is that of the frequent alterations made by the above said government bodies and the lack of awareness of film producers about the various tax shelters available under the law, which make the situation more complicated. Unlike other foreign countries, the governments in India are not providing tax incentives to the various parties associated with the film production.This is also a great hindrance for the growth of the industry. The following table shows the mean scores of the responses of selected film producers towards the Problem of Tax.

Table 4.33 Tests of Between-Subjects Effects

Dependent Variable : Tax

Source	*Type I Sum of Squares*	*Df*	*Mean Square*	*F*	*Sig.*
Type of Ownership in the Company	7304.449	1	7304.449	95.662	***.000****
Producer's Operation	916.745	1	916.745	12.006	***.001****
Experience in Production	1113.588	2	556.794	7.292	***.001****
Error	5726.767	75	76.357		
Total	15061.550	79			

*Significant at 5 per cent level

(Source: Primary data)

Estimated Marginal Means

Table 4.34 Type of Ownership in the Company

Dependent Variable : Tax				
Type of Ownership in the Company	*Mean*	*Std. Error*	*95% Confidence Interval*	
			Lower Bound	*Upper Bound*
Single	28.456	1.471	25.525	31.387
Partnership	**45.190**	3.550	38.118	52.261

(Source: Primary data)

Table 4.35 Producer's Operation

Dependent Variable : Tax				
Producer's Operation	*Mean*	*Std. Error*	*95% Confidence Interval*	
			Lower Bound	*Upper Bound*
Production Only	36.099	3.745	28.639	43.559
Production and Distribution	**37.547**	1.467	34.626	40.469

(Source: Primary data)

Table 4.36 Experience in Production

Dependent Variable : Tax				
Experience in Production	*Mean*	*Std. Error*	*95% Confidence Interval*	
			Lower Bound	*Upper Bound*
11-15 Years	25.642	4.981	15.719	35.566
16-20 Years	39.642	1.731	36.194	43.091
Above 20 Years	**45.184**	1.464	42.267	48.101

(Source: Primary data)

From Tables 4.33, 4.34, 4.35 and 4.36, it may be understood that the problem of tax has much affected producers having a partnership form of ownership in the company (Mean 45.190). At the same time, considering the experience of film producers in production, the producers having above 20 years of experience in production face the problem more seriously than other categories of producers in the industry. Also, the producers concentrating in production and distribution face this problem the most. The mean score variation is found significant at 5 per cent level (P<.05) for all categories of film producers functioning in the industry.

4.3.3 Central Board of Film Certification

One of the most recent issues faced by the film producers functioning in the industry is with regard to the film certification process. There is prevalence of strict rules and regulations in the process of Certification by CBFC.The huge cost and time taken for the film certification are also the major concerns of producers in the industry. A majority of film producers functioning in the industry are unaware of the right certification procedure, which situation also causes delay in the certification procedure. In addition to this the high chance of piracy from CBFC authorities is another major concern for the producers in the industry. The following Table shows the mean scores of the responses of selected film producers towards the Problem of Film Certification.

Table 4.37 Tests of Between-Subjects Effects

Dependent Variable : Central Board of Film Certification

Source	*Type I Sum of Squares*	*Df*	*Mean Square*	*F*	*Sig.*
Type of Ownership in the Company	4809.796	1	4809.796	192.342	*.000**

Producer's Operation	16.132	1	16.132	.645	.424
Experience in Production	641.786	2	320.893	12.832	***.000****
Error	1875.486	75	25.006		
Total	7343.200	79			

*Significant at 5 per cent level

(Source: Primary data)

Estimated Marginal Means

Table 4.38 Type of Ownership in the Company

Dependent Variable : Central Board of Film Certification

Type of Ownership in the Company	*Mean*	*Std. Error*	*95% Confidence Interval*	
			Lower Bound	*Upper Bound*
Single	21.481	.842	19.803	23.158
Partnership	**36.342**	2.031	32.295	40.389

(Source: Primary data)

Table 4.39 Producer's Operation

Dependent Variable : Central Board of Film Certification

Producer's Operation	*Mean*	*Std. Error*	*95% Confidence Interval*	
			Lower Bound	*Upper Bound*
Production Only	27.487	2.143	23.218	31.756
Production and Distribution	**30.335**	.839	28.663	32.007

(Source: Primary data)

Table 4.40 Experience in Production

Dependent Variable : Central Board of Film Certification				
Experience in Production	*Mean*	*Std. Error*	*95% Confidence Interval*	
			Lower Bound	*Upper Bound*
11-15 Years	28.006	2.851	22.327	33.685
16-20 Years	26.006	.991	24.033	27.980
Above 20 Years	**32.721**	.838	31.052	34.391

(Source: Primary data)

Tables 4.37, 4.38, 4.39 and 4.40 depict that the problem of Central Board of Film Certification has much affected producers having a partnership form of ownership in the company (Mean 36.342). At the same time, considering the experience of film producers in production, the producers having above 20 years of experience in production face the problem more seriously than other categories of producers in the industry. Also, the producers concentrating in production and distribution are found to face this problem the more seriously. The mean score variation is found significant at 5 per cent level ($P<.05$) for type of ownership in the production company and experience of the producer in production, but not significant for the producer's movie operation in the industry.

4.3.4 Multiplex

Another major problem encountered by film producers in the industry is the greater concentration of film producers in the multiplexes. A limited number of multiplexes are functioning in the industry, but huge majorities of the audience are attracted towards them. Increased acceptance of visual effects in films by the audience and DTH facilities provided by the multiplexes, have served to increased the demand for multiplex releases rapidly. Lack of knowledge on the part of producers regarding the tax structure for releasing movies in multiplexes and high competition from other language movies in multiplexes are some of the problems faced by film producers in the industry. The following Table shows the mean score of the responses of Selected Film Producers towards the problem of Multiplexes.

Table 4.41 Tests of Between-Subjects Effects

Dependent Variable : Multiplexes

Source	*Type I Sum of Squares*	*Df*	*Mean Square*	*F*	*Sig.*
Type of Ownership in the Company	5843.536	1	5843.536	176.237	***.000****
Producer's Operation	17.829	1	17.829	.538	.466
Experience in Production	508.727	2	254.364	7.671	***.001****
Error	2486.795	75	33.157		
Total	8856.887	79			

*Significant at 5 per cent level

(Source: Primary data)

Estimated Marginal Means

Table 4.42 Type of Ownership in the Company

Dependent Variable : Multiplexes

Type of Ownership in the Company	*Mean*	*Std. Error*	*95% Confidence Interval*	
			Lower Bound	*Upper Bound*
Single	23.141	.970	21.209	25.072
Partnership	**40.475**	2.339	35.815	45.135

(Source: Primary data)

Table 4.43 Producer's Operation

Dependent Variable : Multiplexes

Producer's Operation	*Mean*	*Std. Error*	*95% Confidence Interval*	
			Lower Bound	*Upper Bound*
Production Only	30.997	2.468	26.081	35.913
Production and Distribution	**32.619**	.966	30.693	34.544

(Source: Primary data)

Table 4.44 Experience in Production

Dependent Variable : Multiplexes

Experience in Production	*Mean*	*Std. Error*	*95% Confidence Interval*	
			Lower Bound	*Upper Bound*
11-15 Years	31.856	3.283	25.317	38.395
16-20 Years	28.856	1.141	26.583	31.129
Above 20 Years	**34.711**	.965	32.789	36.633

(Source: Primary data)

Tables 4.41, 4.42, 4.43 and 4.44 depict that the problem of multiplexes has much affected film producers who have a partnership form of ownership in the production company (Mean 40.475). At the same time, considering the experience of film producers in production, the producers having an experience above 20 years face the problem more seriously than other categories of producers in the industry. Also the producers operating in production and distribution faced this problem the most. The mean score variation is found significant at 5 per cent level ($P<.05$) for type of ownership in the production company and experience of producer in production, but not significant for producers' movie operation in the industry.

4.3.5 Competition from Other Entertainment Sectors

Another major problem encountered by film producers in the industry is Competition from Other Entertainment Sectors. Nowadays there is drastic increase in demand for amusement parks, water sports, resorts, etc. The special offers and packages offered by these segments have reduced the demand of the films in theatres. The advertising strategy adopted by these segments has a widespread influence on the audience. Also, the addiction of a majority of audience towards television serials as well as speedy release of movies in television within 3-4 months of movie release in theatres, has made a huge reduction in the theatre crowd. Also, the vast varieties of channels are providing attractive and interesting offers to the audience. All these factors have reduced the demand for films in theatres. The following Table shows the mean scores of the responses of Selected Film Producers the problem of Competition from Other Entertainment Sectors.

Table 4.45 Tests of Between-Subjects Effects

Dependent Variable : Competition from Other Entertainment Sectors

Source	*Type I Sum of Squares*	*Df*	*Mean Square*	*F*	*Sig.*
Type of Ownership in the Company	4873.910	1	4873.910	173.381	***.000****
Producer's Operation	33.261	1	33.261	1.183	.280
Experience in Production	879.892	2	439.946	15.650	***.000****
Error	2108.324	75	28.111		
Total	7895.387	79			

*Significant at 5 per cent level

(Source: Primary data)

Estimated Marginal Means

Table 4.46 Type of Ownership in the Company

Dependent Variable : Competition From Other Entertainment Sectors

Type of Ownership in the Company	*Mean*	*Std. Error*	*95% Confidence Interval*	
			Lower Bound	*Upper Bound*
Single	21.015	.893	19.237	22.794
Partnership	**34.440**	2.154	30.150	38.731

(Source: Primary data)

Table 4.47 Producer's Operation

Dependent Variable : Competition From Other Entertainment Sectors

Producer's Operation	*Mean*	*Std. Error*	*95% Confidence Interval*	
			Lower Bound	*Upper Bound*
Production Only	24.846	2.272	20.319	29.372
Production and Distribution	**30.610**	.890	28.837	32.383

(Source: Primary data)

Table 4.48 Experience in Production

Dependent Variable : Competition From Other Entertainment Sectors

Experience in Production	*Mean*	*Std. Error*	*95% Confidence Interval*	
			Lower Bound	*Upper Bound*
11-15 Years	27.830	3.022	21.809	33.851
16-20 Years	23.830	1.050	21.738	25.923
Above 20 Years	**31.523**	.888	29.753	33.293

(Source: Primary data)

Tables 4.45, 4.46, 4.47 and 4.48 depict that the problem of Competition from Other Entertainment Sectors has much affected film producers who have a partnership form of ownership in the production company (Mean 34.440). At the same time, considering the experience of film producers in production, the producers having an experience of above 20 years face the problem more than other categories of producers in the industry. Also, the producers operating in production and distribution face this problem seriously. The mean score variation is found significant at 5 per cent level (P<.05) for type of ownership in the production company and experience of producer in production, but not significant for producers concentrating with movie operation in the industry.

4.4 Discriminant Analysis – Single / Partnership

Here, multiple discriminant analysis is used to identify the most critical problem that affects the film producers of Malayalam film industry owning single and partnership companies. The output of multiple discriminant analysis is presented in Tables 4.49, 4.50 and 4.51.

Table 4.49 Wilks' Lambda

Test of Function(s)	*Wilks' Lambda*	*Chi-square*	*Df*	*Sig.*
1	.194	121.999	7	*.000**

*Significant at 5 per cent level
(Source: Primary data)

Table 4.50 Functions at Group Centroids

Type of Ownership in the Company	*Function*
	1
Single	-1.818
Partnership	2.222

(Unstandardized canonical discriminant functions evaluated at group means)

Table 4.51 Standardized Canonical Discriminant Function Coefficients

	Function
	1
Difficulty in obtaining government grants	.300
Cast and CrewStory	1.008-.208
Focus on Stardom	-1.457
Copyright and Intellectual Property Rights	**-1.694**
Difficulty in Identification and Obtaining of Sources of Funds	**2.607**
Visual Effects Industry	-.546

The Wilks Lambda Matrix (Table 4.49) of Discriminant Analysis gives a statistically significant Chi- square value (values of Chi-square **121.999with p=000<.05**), which means that the discriminant function for identifying the most critical problem of film producers functioning in Malayalam film industry is valid.

From the function at group centroids (Table 4.50) negative coefficients are found for problems of film producers having single ownership in companies and positive coefficients are for the problems of film producers having partnership ownership in companies. Therefore, from the standardized canonical discriminant function coefficient matrix (Table 4.51), it can be observed that Difficulty in Identification and Obtaining of Sources of Funds **(2.607)**, Cast and Crew **(1.008)** and Difficulty in Obtaining Government Grants **(.300)** have the highest positive coefficients. Similarly, Copyright and Intellectual Property Rights **(-1.694)** and Focus on Stardom **(-1.457)** have the highest negative coefficients.

Therefore, as per the coefficient in the group centroid matrix and Standardized Canonical Discriminant Function matrix, it can be concluded that Difficulty in Identification and Obtaining of Sources of Funds are the most vital problem faced by film producers having partnership ownership in companies followed by Cast and Crew and Difficulty in obtaining Government grants, whereas Copyright and Intellectual Property Rights is the most important problem faced by film producers having single ownership in companies, followed by Focus on Stardom and Visual Effects Industry.

4.5 Discriminant Analysis – Production Only / Production and Distribution

Here, multiple discriminant analysis is used to identify the most critical problem that affects the film producers of Malayalam film industry concentrating either in production only or in production and distribution. The output of multiple discriminant analysis is presented in Tables 4.52, 4.53 and 4.54.

Table 4.52 Wilks' Lambda

Test of Function(s)	*Wilks' Lambda*	*Chi-square*	*Df*	*Sig.*
1	.100	171.399	7	***.000****

*Significant at 5 per cent level

(Source: Primary data)

Table 4.53 Functions at Group Centroids

Producer's Operation	*Function*
	1
Production Only	-3.820
Production and Distribution	2.292

(Unstandardized canonical discriminant functions evaluated at group means)

Table 4.54 Standardized Canonical Discriminant Function Coefficients

	Function
	1
Difficulty in Obtaining Government Grant	-2.860
Cast and CrewStory	1.044.883
Focus on Stardom	.383
Copyright and Intellectual Property Rights	**-6.026**
Difficulty in Identification and Obtaining of Sources of Fund	**8.258**
Visual Effects Industry	-1.183

(Unstandardized canonical discriminant functions evaluated at group means)

The Wilks Lambda Matrix (Table 4.52) of Discriminant Analysis gives a statistically significant Chi- square value (values of Chi-square **171.399 with p=000<.05**), which means the discriminant function for identifying the most critical problem of film producers functioning in Malayalam film industry is valid.

From the function at group centroids (Table 4.53), negative coefficients are found for film producers concentrating in production only, and positive coefficients are found for film producers concentrating in production and distribution. Therefore from the standardized canonical discriminant function coefficient matrix (Table 4.54), it can be observed that Difficulties in the Identification and Obtaining of Sources of Fund **(8.258)**, Cast and Crew **(1.044)** and Story **(.883)** have the highest positive coefficients. Similarly, Copyright and Intellectual Property Rights**(-6.026)** and Difficulty in obtaining government grants**(-2.860)** have the highest negative coefficients.

Therefore, as per the coefficients in the group centroid matrix and Standardized Canonical Discriminant Function matrix, it is can be concluded that Difficulty in the Identification and Obtaining of Sources of Funds is the most vital problem faced by film producers operating in production and distribution, followed by Cast and Crew and Story, whereas Copyright and Intellectual Property Rights is the most important problem faced by film producers operating in production only, followed by Difficulty in Obtaining Government Grants and Visual Effects Industry.

4.6 Analysis of Production Problems (Experience Production-wise)

When responses to Difficulty in obtaining Government Grants, Cast and Crew, Story, Focus on Stardom, Copyright and Intellectual Property Rights, Difficulty in the Identification and Obtaining of Sources of Funds, Visual Effects Industry, Piracy, Tax, Central Board of Film Certification, Multiplexes and Competition from Other Entertainment Sectors are observed among the selected film producershaving production experience of 11-15 years, 16-20 years and above 20 years, the following summary is obtained.

From Table 4.55, it is evident that the problems related to Difficulty in Obtaining GovernmentGrants, Copyright and Intellectual Property Rights, Difficulty inthe Identification and Obtaining of Sources of Funds, Tax, Central Board of Film Certification, Multiplex and Competition from Other Entertainment Sectors are faced more by film producers having a production experience of above 20 years. At the same time, problems related to Focus on Stardom, Visual Effects Industry and Piracy are faced more by film producers having a production experience of 11–15 years. Also, it can be inferred that problems of Cast and Crew and Story are seen high for producers with production experience ranging from 16-20 years.

Table 4.55 Showing Group Statistics for Production Problems

Experience in Production		Difficulty in obtaining Government Grant	Cast and Crew	Story	Focus on Stardom	Copyright and Property Rights	Difficulty in Identification and Obtaining of Sources of Fund	Visual Effects Industry	Piracy	Tax	Central Board of Film Certification	Multiplexes	Competition from Other Entertainment Sectors
11-15 Years	Mean	45.0	24.0	14.0	63.0	25.0	30.0	20.0	45.0	18.0	22.0	34.0	34.0
	N	7	7	7	7	7	7	7	7	7	7	7	7
	Std. Deviation	.00	.00	.00	.00	.00	.00	.00	.00	.00	.00	.00	.00
16-20 Years	Mean	44.6	25.4	29.7	30.7	27.1	28.5	19.4	44.2	41.9	28.5	31.2	27.0
	N	36	36	36	36	36	36	36	36	36	36	36	36
	Std. Deviation	19.62	9.44	13.63	10.03	12.70	14.17	10.57	16.83	11.75	10.17	12.77	12.74
Above 20 Years	Mean	46.7	20.2	29.2	29.4	32.1	31.5	18.9	41.7	42.9	30.5	32.4	29.1
	N	37	37	37	37	37	37	37	37	37	37	37	37
	Std. Deviation	17.50	11.24	12.84	8.05	8.08	10.81	5.00	16.21	13.33	9.53	8.70	8.26
Total	Mean	45.6	22.9	28.1	32.9	28.7	30.0	19.2	43.1	40.3	28.9	31.1	27.7
	N	80	80	80	80	80	80	80	80	80	80	80	80
	Std. Deviation	17.64	10.1	13.30	12.73	10.36	12.02	8.12	15.71	13.80	9.64	10.58	5.95

The results of the One-way ANOVA are depicted in the following Table.

Table 4.56 ANOVA Table

		Sum of Squares	*Df*	*Mean Squares*	*F*	*Sig.*
Difficulty in Obtaining	Between Groups (Combined)	80.903	2	40.451	**.127**	.881
Government	Within Groups	24509.297	77	318.303		
Grants	Total	24590.200	79			
Cast and Crew	Between Groups (Combined)	497.098	2	248.549	**2.492**	.089
	Within Groups	7678.702	77	99.723		
	Total	8175.800	79			
Story	Between Groups (Combined)	1542.408	2	771.204	**4.773**	***.011****
	Within Groups	12442.480	77	161.591		
	Total	13984.887	79			
Focus on Stardom	Between Groups (Combined)	6957.497	2	3478.748	**45.802**	***.000****
	Within Groups	5848.303	77	75.952		
	Total	12805.800	79			
Copyright and Intellectual	Between Groups (Combined)	832.508	2	416.254	**4.191**	***.019****
Property Rights	Within Groups	7647.880	77	99.323		
	Total	8480.388	79			
Difficulty in Identification &	Between Groups (Combined)	168.698	2	84.349	**.578**	.564
Obtaining of	Within Groups	11246.189	77	146.054		
Sources of Funds	Total	11414.888	79			

Visual Effects Industry	Between Groups (Combined)	8.358	2	4.179	**.062**	.940
	Within Groups	5208.642	77	67.645		
	Total	5217.000	79			
Piracy	Between Groups (Combined)	136.530	2	68.265	**.271**	.763
	Within Groups	19381.020	77	251.702		
	Total	19517.550	79			
Tax	Between Groups (Combined)	3842.688	2	1921.344	**13.187**	***.000****
	Within Groups	11218.862	77	145.700		
	Total	15061.550	79			
Central Board of Film Certification	Between Groups (Combined)	441.147	2	220.573	**2.461**	.092
	Within Groups	6902.053	77	89.637		
	Total	7343.200	79			
Multiplexes	Between Groups (Combined)	416.746	2	208.373	**1.901**	.156
	Within Groups	8440.141	77	109.612		
	Total	8856.887	79			
Competition From Other Entertainment Sectors	Between Groups (Combined)	190.962	2	95.481	**.954**	.390
	Within Groups	7704.426	77	100.057		
	Total	7895.387	79			

(Source: Primary data)*Significant at 5 per cent level

From the above Tables, it is evident from the mean scoresof responses of selected film producers on the Difficulty in Obtaining Government Grants that producers having above 20 years of production experience and producers having production experience in between 11-15 years face the problem more seriously than other categories of producers in the industry. The highest mean score is that of producers having above 20 years of production experience (**Mean 46.7**) and 11-15 years of experience (**Mean 45.0**). Also, the mean score variation isnot statistically significant at 5 per cent level (**value of F = .127 with P = .881>.05**). So it can be concluded that there is no difference in the mean scores obtained for government grants-related problems.

The mean score responses of Cast and Crew related problems revealthat the producers having an experience of 16-20 years and 11-15 years face this problem more seriously. The highest mean scores are those of producers having a production experience of 16-20 years **(Mean score 25.4),** followed by film producers having 11-15 years of experience. Also, the mean score variation is not statistically significant at 5 per cent level (**value of F = 2.492 with P = .089>.05).** So, it can be inferred that there is no difference in the mean scores obtained for Cast and Crew-related problems.

From the above Tables, it is clear that producers having a production experience of 16-20 years have faced Story-related problems more seriously than any other category of producers. The highest mean scores are obtained for film producers having production experience of 16-20 years (**Mean 29.7**) and above 20 years (**Mean 12.3810**). The mean score variation is statistically significant at 5 per cent level (Value of **F = 4.773 with P=0.011<.05**). Thus, it may be concluded that there is difference in the mean scores obtained for Story-related production problems.

Based on the mean score responses of selected film producers on Focus on Stardom related problems, producers having production experience in between 11-15 years and producers who are having above 20 years of production experience are found to face the problem more seriously. The highest mean score was that of producers having 11-15 yearsof experience (**Mean score 63.0**) and producers having 16-20 yearsof experience (**Mean score 30.7**). The mean score variation is statistically significant at 5 per cent level (**value of F = 45.802 with P = .000<.05**). So, it can be concluded that there is difference in the mean scores obtained for Focus on Stardom - related problems.

The above Tables also reveal that Copyright and Intellectual Property Rights related problems highly affect producers having production experience of above 20 years with a**Mean score of 33.1,** followed by film producers having production experience of 16-20 years and 11-15 years. The mean score variation is statistically significant at 5 per cent level (Value of **F = 4.191 with P=0.019<.05**). Thus, it can be concluded that there is difference in the mean scores obtained for Copyright and Intellectual Property Rights-related problems.

Regarding problems inObtaining of Sources of Fund related, producers having production experience of above 20 yearsare found to face more serious problems than any other category of film producers. The highest mean scores are those for producers having above 20 years ofproduction experience (**Mean score 31.5**) and 11-15 yearsof production experience (**Mean score 30.0**). The mean score variation is not statistically significant at 5 per cent level (Value of **F = .578 with P=0.564>.05**), which implies that there is no difference in the mean scores obtained for the Difficulty in Obtaining of Sources of Funds.

The mean score responses of Visual Effects Industry related problems reveal that the producers having an experience of 11-15 years and 16-20 years face this problem seriously. The highest mean scores are those of producers having a production experience of 11-15 years **(Mean 20.0),** followed by film producers having 16-20 yearsof experience. Also, the mean score variation is not statistically significant at 5 per cent level (**value of F = .062 with P = .940>.05).** So, it can be inferred that there is no difference in the mean scores obtained for Visual Effects Industry-related problems.

Based on the mean score responses of selected film producers on the Piracy- related problems, producers having production experience of 11-15 years and producers having production experience ranging between 16-20 years are found to face the problem more seriously than other categories of producers in the industry. The highest mean score was that of producers having 11-15 years of production experience (**Mean 45.0**) and 16-20 yearsof experience (**Mean 44.2**), Also, the mean score variation is not statistically significant at 5 per cent level (**value ofF = .271 with P = .763>.05**). So, it can be concluded that there is no difference in the mean scores obtained for Piracy-related problems.

By analyzing the above Tables, it can be inferred that Tax-related problems highly affectproducers having production experience of above 20 years with a **Mean** of **42.9,** followed by film producers having production experience of 16-20 years and 11-15 years. The mean score variation is statistically significant at 5 per cent level (Value of **F = 13.187 with P=0.000<.05**). Thus it can be concluded that there is difference in the mean scores obtained for Tax-related problems.

When considering the central board of film certification related problems, producers having production experience of above 20 yearsare found to face more serious problems than any other category of film producers. The highest mean scores are those for producers having above 20 years of production experience (Mean 30.5) and 16-20 years of production experience (Mean **28.5**). The mean score variation is not statistically significant at 5 per cent level (Value of **F = 2.461 with P=0.092>.05**), which implies that there is no difference in the mean scores obtained for Central Board of Film Certification-related problems.

From the above tables it can be inferred that multiplexes-related problems highly affect producers having production experience of above 20 years with **Mean of 32.4,** followed by film producers having production experience of 16-20 years and 11-15 years. The mean score variation is not statistically significant at 5 per cent level (Value of **F = 1.901 with P=.156>.05**). Thus, it can be concluded that there is no difference in the mean scores obtained for Multiplex-related problems.

The mean score responses of Competition from Other Entertainment Sectors-related problems reveal that producers having an experience of above 20 years and 16-20 years face this problem more seriously. The highest mean scores arethose of producers having a production experience of above 20 years **(Mean score 29.1),** followed by film producers having 16-20 years of experience. The mean score variation is not statistically significant at 5 per cent level (**value of F = .954 with P =.390>.05).** So it can be inferred that there is no difference in the mean scores obtained for Competition from Other Entertainment Sectors related problems.

4.7 Conclusion

This chapter deals with the various production and marketing problems faced by film producers in the industry. The important problems faced by producers in the production of movies include Difficulty in obtaining Government Grants, Cast and Crew, Story, Focus on Stardom, Copyright and Intellectual Property Rights, Difficulty in the Identification and Obtaining of Sources of Fund and Visual Effects (VFX) Industry. The major marketing problems faced by them include Piracy, Tax, CBFC (Central Board of Film Certification), Multiplexes and Competition from Other Segments of the Entertainment Sector.

By making use of the Canonical Discriminant Function matrix, it can be concluded that Difficulty in the Identification and Obtaining of Sources of Funds is the most vital problem faced by film producers having partnership ownership in companies followed by Cast and Crew and Difficulty in Obtaining Government Grants, whereas Copyright and Intellectual Property Rights is the most important problem faced by film producers having single ownership in companies, followed by Focus on Stardom and Visual Effects Industry. Also, from the study it can be inferred that Difficulty in Identification and Obtaining of Sources of Funds is the most vital problem faced by film producers operating in production and distribution, followed by Cast and Crew and Story, whereas Copyright and Intellectual Property Rights is the most important problem faced by film producers operating in production only, followed by Difficulty in Obtaining Government Grants and Visual Effects Industry. The study also reveals that the problems related to Difficulty in Obtaining Government Grants, Copyright and Intellectual Property Rights, Difficulty in Identification and Obtaining of Sources of Fund, Tax, Central Board of Film Certification, Multiplex and Competition from Other Entertainment Sectors are hurdles faced more by film producers having a production experience of above 20 years. At the same time, problems related to Focus on Stardom, Visual Effects Industry and Piracy are faced more by film producers having a production experience of 11–15 years. Also, the problems relating to Cast and Crew and Story are seen high for producers with production experience ranging from 16-20 years.

REFERENCES

[1] Andy Field. (2010). *Discovering Statistics Using SAS Software*, 11-28.

[2] David Silverman. (2010). *Quantitative Research*, Sage Publishers, 13-31.

[3] Erich Lechman., & George. (1998). *Theory of Point Estimation*, 11-22.

[4] Joseph Hair. (2010). *Multivariate Data Analysis*, Pearson Publication, 2-16.

[5] Kumar Pranab. (1986). *Contemporary Text Book on Statistical Analysis*, 480-549.

[6] Liese. & Klaus. (2008). *Statistical Decision Theory*, 21-34.

[7] Mark J. (1987). *Review of Multivariate Analysis*, 391-411.

[8] Peter J. (2001). *Mathematical Statistics*, 16-38.

[9] Robert Torrie. (1977). *Principles and Procedures of Statistics*, 22-36.

[10] Stiglerr, Stephen M. (1978). *Mathematical Statistics in Early States*, 190-216.

[11] Wald, Abraham. (1947). *Sequential Analysis*, 18-57.

5

Problems of Cine Distributors in Kerala

The cine distributors functioning in the Malayalam film industry are facing enormous problems in the distribution of films. The problems faced by them may differon the basis of type of films distributed, experience of distributors in this field, concentration of distributors in certain language films, etc. In addition to this, the problem also differs on the basis of promotion tools used by distributors for their film distribution. The major marketing problems encountered by them include increased tax rates, difficulty in the obtainment of various grants from the government, disputes that are arising between various cine distributors' associations prevailing in the industry,etc. Also, the various charges and fees imposed by government authorities from time to time, difficulty in the obtainment of institutional funds from banks and other financial institutions for expanding their distribution channel,etc, are other problems encountered.

Here, in order to study in detail about the marketing problems faced by cine distributors in the Malayalam film industry, 310 cine distributors are selected from a total population of 904, by applying the simple random sampling method. Out of the sample of 310, 128 cine distributors are focused in the distribution of Malayalam movies, 96 in the distribution of Hindi movies, and 86 in the distribution of Tamil movies. When considering the experience in film distribution, approximately half the percentage of distributors functioning in the industry (49.4 percent) have an experience in film distribution, ranging from 16-20 years.

A structured questionnaire is designed and distributed and data is collected from 310 selected distributors. Various problems of distribution such as Association, Tax, Multiplex, Difficulty in the Obtainment of Government Grants and Competition from Other Segments of Entertainment Sector are taken into account inorder to study in detail about the marketing problems faced by the cine exhibitors in Malayalam movie industry.

Various statistical techniques such as Friedman Test, Kruskal Wallis Test,One Way- ANOVA are also being used inorder to understand in detail the level of these problems, according to certain objects and how the problems are related to each other, etc.

5.1 Frequency Distribution of the Film Distributors Selected for the Study

The following Tables, 5.1, 5.2 and 5.3, show the selected film distributors' concentration in film distribution, film distributors' experience in film distribution, and type of films distributed by distributors.

Table 5.1 Concentration in Film Distribution

	Frequency	*Percentage*	*Valid Percentage*	*Cumulative Percentage*
Malayalam	128	41.3	41.3	41.3
Hindi	96	31.0	31.0	72.3
Tamil	86	27.7	27.7	100.0
Total	310	100.0	100.0	

(Source: Primary data)

Table 5.2 Experience in Film Distribution

	Frequency	*Percentage*	*Valid Percentage*	*Cumulative Percentage*
11-15 Years	61	19.7	19.7	19.7
16-20 Years	153	49.4	49.4	69.0
Above 20	96	31.0	31.0	100.0
Total	310	100.0	100.0	

(Source: Primary data)

Table 5.3 Type of Films Distributed by the Company

	Frequency	*Percentage*	*Valid Percentage*	*Cumulative Percentage*
Adventure	153	49.4	49.4	49.4
Comedy	93	30.0	30.0	79.4
Crime	32	10.3	10.3	89.7
Epics/Historical	32	10.3	10.3	100.0
Total	310	100.0	100.0	

(Source: Primary data)

From the Table 5.1, it is clear that 41.3 per cent of the selected cine distributors are concentrating in the distribution of Malayalam movies, 31 per cent in the distribution of Hindi movie and 27.7 per cent in the distribution of Tamil movies. So, it can he concluded that the majority of the cine distributors functioning in the industry are concentrating in Malayalam movie distribution. When analyzing Table 5.2, it is evident that 49.4 per cent of the selected cine distributors functioning in the industry have an experience in film distribution ranging from 16-20 years, followed by above 20 years of experience and 11-15 years of experience. So it can be concluded that the majority of the distributors functioning in the industry are having an experience of 16-20 years. Also from Table 5.3, it is observed that 49.4 per cent of the selected distributors functioning in the industry are concentrating in the distribution of adventure type movies, followed by distributors concentrating in comedy-focused movies. The distributors focusing in crime and epic movies amount to 10.3 percent each in the movie distribution. So, it is concluded that the majority the film distributors in industry are of focusing on adventure-oriented movies.

5.2 Marketing Problems of Cine Distributors

5.2.1 Tax

The most serious problem faced by cine distributors in the industry is the burden of tax. The taxes are imposed by the Central Government, State Government as well as the local bodies like municipalities and panchayaths. The Government levies tax in the form of sales tax, entertainment tax, distribution tax, service tax, etc. The rates of tax levied by these government bodies are also of great difference. Another most important problem in tax is the frequent alterations made by the abovesaid bodies and the lack of awareness of cine distributors about the various tax shelters available under the law which makes the situation more complicated. Unlike other foreign countries, the governments are not providing tax incentives to the various parties associated with the film distribution, which is also a great hindrance for the growth of the industry. The following table shows the mean scores of the responses of selected Cine Distributors towards the Problem of Tax.

Table 5.4 Tests of Between-Subjects Effects

Dependent Variable: Tax					
Source	*Type I Sum of Squares*	*Df*	*Mean Square*	*F*	*Sig.*
Concentration in Film distribution	24617.356	2	12308.678	1904.523	***.000****
Experience in Film Distribution	1009.163	2	504.581	78.074	***.000****
Error	1971.175	305	6.463		
Total	27597.694	309			

*Significant at 5 per cent level

(Source: Primary data)

Estimated Marginal Means

Table 5.5 Concentration in Film Distribution

Dependent Variable: Tax				
Concentration in Film Distribution	*Mean*	*Std. Error*	*95% Confidence Interval*	
			Lower Bound	*Upper Bound*
Malayalam	41.696	.232	41.238	42.153
Hindi	20.959	.293	20.382	21.536
Tamil	33.693	.300	33.102	34.284

(Source: Primary data)

Table 5.6 Experience in Film Distribution

Dependent Variable: Tax				
Experience in Film Distribution	*Mean*	*Std. Error*	*95% Confidence Interval*	
			Lower Bound	*Upper Bound*
11-15 Years	34.946	.344	34.269	35.623
16-20 Years	32.069	.210	31.657	32.482
Above 20 Years	29.332	.291	28.760	29.905

(Source: Primary data)

As per Tables 5.4, 5.5 and 5.6, it may be understood that the problem of tax is very high for distributors concentrating in Malayalam movies (Mean 41.696); also,considering the experience in distribution, the distributors havingan experience of 11-15 years, face this problem more seriously than distributors having an experience of 16-20 years and above 20 years of distribution experience. The mean score variation is found significant at 5 per cent level ($P<.05$) for all categories of cine distributors functioning in the industry.

5.2.2 Association

Another major problem encountered by cine distributors in the industry is the lack of coordination between the various cine distributors' associations. There is the prevalence of various registered and unregistered cine distributors' associations functioning in the industry. The frequent conflicts arising in between these associations are also a great problem. Often, a large number of associationsis preventing the distribution of certain movies in certain classes of theatres, which makes the situation worse; also, the difference of opinion of various associations regarding these issues is also of great concern to the industry. Even though the government has formulated various policies in solving these problems, thefinal results of these policies are not meeting the target. The following Tables show the mean scores of the responses of the selected Cine Distributors towards the problem of Association.

Table 5.7 Tests of Between-Subjects Effects

Dependent Variable: Association

Source	*Type I Sum of Squares*	*Df*	*Mean Square*	*F*	*Sig.*
Concentration in Film Distribution	20563.063	2	10281.531	537.785	***.000****
Experience in Film Distribution	10.782	2	5.391	.282	.754
Error	5831.074	305	19.118		
Total	26404.919	309			

**Significant at 5 per cent level*

(Source: Primary data)

Estimated Marginal Means

Table 5.8 Concentration in Film Distribution

Dependent Variable: Association

Concentration in Film Distribution	*Mean*	*Std. Error*	*95% Confidence Interval*	
			Lower Bound	*Upper Bound*
Malayalam	**43.059**	.400	42.272	43.845
Hindi	23.586	.504	22.593	24.579
Tamil	35.529	.516	34.513	36.546

(Source: Primary data)

Table 5.9 Experience in Film Distribution

Dependent Variable: Association				
Experience in Film Distribution	*Mean*	*Std. Error*	*95% Confidence Interval*	
			Lower Bound	*Upper Bound*
11-15 Years	34.054	.591	32.891	35.218
16-20 Years	34.296	.360	33.587	35.005
Above 20 Years	33.824	.501	32.839	34.809

(Source: Primary data)

Tables 5.7, 5.8, and 5.9, indicate that the problem of Association is very high for film distributors who are concentrating more in Malayalam movies (Mean 43.059). At the same time, considering the experience in film distribution, distributors having an experience of 16-20 years face more problem seriously than other categories of distributors in the industry. The mean score variation is found significant at 5 per cent level for concentration in film distribution (P<.05), but not significant for experience in film distribution (P>.05).

5.2.3 *Multiplexes*

Another major problem encountered by cine distributors in the industry is the greater concentration of film producers for multiplexes release. A limited number of multiplexes are functioning in the industry, but a large number ofaudiences are attracted towards it. Increased acceptance of visual effects in films by the audience, and DTH facilities provided by the multiplexes, have increased the demand for multiplex releases rapidly. Even though huge ticket prices are charged from the audience in the multiplexes, and there is a great difference of tax in the release of movies in multiplexes, when compared to local theatres, the multiplex owners are able to fill the hall before the commencement of shows. The huge cost incurred in the distribution of movies in multiplexes, besides the accomplishment of several legal formalities for distribution in multiplexes, is a major headache for the film distributors in multiplex releases. The following Table show the mean scores of the responses of selected Cine Exhibitors towards the problem of Multiplex.

Table 5.10 Tests of Between-Subjects Effects

Dependent Variable: Multiplex

Source	*Type I Sum of Squares*	*Df*	*Mean Square*	*F*	*Sig.*
Concentration in Film Distribution	27288.431	2	13644.215	3251.110	***.000****
Experience in Film Distribution	2513.836	2	1256.918	299.495	***.000****
Error	1280.020	305	4.197		
Total	31082.287	309			

**Significant at 5 per cent level of significance*

(Source: Primary data)

Estimated Marginal Means

Table 5.11 Concentration in Film Distribution

Dependent Variable: Multiplex

Concentration in Film Distribution	*Mean*	*Std. Error*	*95% Confidence Interval*	
			Lower Bound	*Upper Bound*
Malayalam	39.433	.187	39.065	39.802
Hindi	20.335	.236	19.870	20.800
Tamil	37.797	.242	37.320	38.273

(Source: Primary data)

Table 5.12 Experience in Film Distribution

Dependent Variable: Multiplex				
Experience in Film Distribution	*Mean*	*Std. Error*	*95% Confidence Interval*	
			Lower Bound	*Upper Bound*
11-15 Years	34.391	.277	33.846	34.936
16-20 Years	28.386	.169	28.054	28.719
Above 20 Years	**34.788**	.235	34.326	35.249

(Source: Primary data)

As per Tables 5.10, 5.11 and 5.12, it is clear that the problem of multiplex is very high in A class theatres (Mean 19.366), and that the exhibitors who concentrate on Malayalam film industry are facing much difficulty (Mean 24.658). With regard to multiplexes, exhibitors having more than 20 years of experience in film exhibition face much problem with regard to multiplexes (Mean 19.948). The mean score variation is found significant at 5 per cent level ($P<.05$) for all categories of cine distributors.

5.2.4 Competition from Other Entertainment Sectors

The major issue faced by cine distributors in the industry is the immense competition faced from other segments of the entertainment sector, including amusement parks, resorts, water sports, etc. Special offers and packages provided by these segments have created a huge demand among the public. Public addiction towards television serials and reality shows, which are also a major segment in the entertainment sector are other hurdles to distributors. Speedy release of movies in television channels within two to three months after movie release in theatres and possibility of watching movies at home, simultaneously with the time of movie release in theatres, are also great concerns to the distributors in the industry. The following

Table shows the mean scores of the responses of Selected Cine Exhibitors towards the problem of competition from other entertainment sectors.

Table 5.13 Tests of Between-Subjects Effects

Dependent Variable: Competition from Other Entertainment Sectors

Source	*Type I Sum of Squares*	*Df*	*Mean Square*	*F*	*Sig.*
Concentration in Film Distribution	18756.499	2	9378.249	4359.445	***.000****
Experience in Film Distribution	52.858	2	26.429	12.285	***.000****
Error	656.131	305	2.151		
Total	19465.487	309			

*Significant at 5 per cent level

(Source: Primary data)

Estimated Marginal Means

Table 5.14 Concentration in Film Distribution

Dependent Variable: Competition from Other Entertainment Sectors

Concentration in Film Distribution	*Mean*	*Std. Error*	*95% Confidence Interval*	
			Lower Bound	*Upper Bound*
Malayalam	**33.917**	.134	33.653	34.181
Hindi	16.167	.169	15.834	16.500
Tamil	30.760	.173	30.419	31.101

(Source: Primary data)

Table 5.15 Experience in Film Distribution

Dependent Variable: Competition from Other Entertainment Sectors				
Experience in Film Distribution	*Mean*	*Std. Error*	*95% Confidence Interval*	
			Lower Bound	*Upper Bound*
11-15 Years	27.532	.198	27.142	27.922
16-20 Years	27.031	.121	26.793	27.268
Above 20 Years	26.281	.168	25.951	26.611

(Source: Primary data)

From Tables 5.13, 14 and 15, it can be concluded that competition from other entertainment sectors affect the functioning of distributors who are concentrating more in Malayalam movies (Mean 33.917), followed by Tamil movies and Hindi movies with Means 30.760 and 16.167 respectively. Based on experience in film distribution the distributors having a distribution experience of 11-15 years are found to face the problem more seriously than other categories of distributors in the industry. The mean score variation is found significant at 5 per cent level of significance ($P<.05$) for all categories of cine distributors.

5.2.5 Difficulty in obtaining of Government Grants

Another major issue faced by cine distributors in the industry is the difficulty in the obtaining of Government grants for movies distributed. The shortage of financial support from the State and Central governments in the form of grants for movie distribution, and the prevalence of strict rules in force for the distribution of these grants,are major problems for cine distributors functioning in the industry. Also, huge delay incurred in the sanctioning and distribution of these grants, distribution of grants only for certain types of movies distributed in the industry, and difference in laws between Central and State governments in providing grants are also other problem affecting the distributors. The following Table shows the mean scores of the responses of selected Cine Distributors towards the Difficulty in the obtainment of Government grants.

Table 5.16 Tests of Between-Subjects Effects

Dependent Variable: Difficulty in Obtaining Government Grants

Source	*Type I Sum of Squares*	*Df*	*Mean Square*	*F*	*Sig.*
Concentration in Film Distribution	23426.839	2	11713.419	7398.645	***.000****
Experience in Film Distribution	703.129	2	351.564	222.062	***.000****
Error	482.871	305	1.583		
Total	24612.839	309			

**Significant at 5 per cent level*

(Source: Primary data)

Estimated Marginal Means

Table 5.17 Concentration in Film Distribution

Dependent Variable: Difficulty in Obtaining Government Grants

Concentration in Film Distribution	*Mean*	*Std. Error*	*95% Confidence Interval*	
			Lower Bound	*Upper Bound*
Malayalam	38.842	.115	38.616	39.069
Hindi	20.421	.145	20.135	20.707
Tamil	36.510	.149	36.217	36.802

(Source: Primary data)

Table 5.18 Experience in Film Distribution

Dependent Variable: Difficulty in Obtaining Government Grants

Experience in Film Distribution	*Mean*	*Std. Error*	*95% Confidence Interval*	
			Lower Bound	*Upper Bound*
11-15 Years	34.240	.170	33.905	34.575
16-20 Years	29.977	.104	29.773	30.181
Above 20 Years	31.556	.144	31.272	31.839

(Source: Primary data)

Tables 5.16, 17 and 18, reveal that the difficulty in obtaining Government grants has much affected film distributors who are concentrating more in Malayalam movies (Mean38.842), followed by Tamil movies and Hindi movies with mean scores 36.510 and 20.421 respectively. Distributors having a distribution experience of 11-15 years are found to facethe problem more seriously than other categories of cine distributors functioning in the industry. The mean scores of other categories are 31.556 and 29.977 for above 20 years of experience and 16-20 years of experience respectively. The mean score variation is found significant at 5 per cent level ($P<.05$) for all categories of cine distributors.

5.3 Marketing Problems According to Experience in Film Distribution

To test whether there is any variation in the mean scores for marketing problems such as tax, association, multiplex, competition from other entertainment sectors, and difficulty in obtaining of government grants, according to experience of film distributors in distribution, a One-way ANOVA has been attempted. The results are shown in Tables 5.19 and 5.20.

Table 5.19 Summary of multiple comparison of Marketing Problem variables with Experience in Film Distribution

Dependent Variable (Marketing Problems)	*Independent Variable (Experience in Distribution)*	*Mean*	*Std. Deviation*
Tax	0-5 Years	31.9477	10.29422
	6-10 Years	29.6882	9.18645
	11-15 Years	37.0000	.00000
	16-20 Years	41.0000	.00000
	Total	32.7258	9.45055
Association	0-5 Years	32.8366	7.63859
	6-10 Years	31.6237	10.05195
	11-15 Years	46.0000	.00000
	16-20 Years	44.0000	.00000
	Total	34.9839	9.24407
Multiplex	0-5 Years	31.1634	8.95784
	6-10 Years	26.4624	9.81188
	11-15 Years	43.0000	.00000
	16-20 Years	42.0000	.00000
	Total	32.0935	10.02945
Competition from OtherEntertainment Sectors	0-5 Years	25.7582	7.55508
	6-10 Years	26.5591	9.46557
	11-15 Years	32.0000	.00000
	16-20 Years	34.0000	.00000
	Total	27.4935	7.93695
Difficulty in Obtaining Government	0-5 Years	30.0850	10.42135
	6-10 Years	29.9032	6.59721

Grants	11-15 Years	39.0000	.00000
	16-20 Years	39.0000	.00000
	Total	31.8710	8.92486

(Source: Primary data)

Table 5.20 Results of One-way ANOVA for Marketing Problems

ANOVA

		Sum of Squares	*Df*	*Mean Squares*	*F*	*Sig.*
Tax	Between Groups	3726.155	3	1242.052	15.921	***.000****
	Within Groups	23871.539	306	78.012		
	Total	27597.694	309			
Association	Between Groups	8240.176	3	2746.725	46.271	***.000****
	Within Groups	18164.743	306	59.362		
	Total	26404.919	309			
Multiplex	Between Groups	10028.254	3	3342.751	48.584	***.000****
	Within Groups	21054.033	306	68.804		
	Total	31082.287	309			
Competition fromother Entertainment Sectors	Between Groups	2546.510	3	848.837	15.352	***.000****
	Within Groups	16918.977	306	55.291		
	Total	19465.487	309			
Difficulty in Obtaining Govt. Grants	Between Groups	4100.814	3	1366.938	20.392	***.000****
	Within Groups	20512.024	306	67.033		
	Total	24612.839	309			

*Significant at 5 per cent level

(Source: Primary data)

The results of the One-Way ANOVA for the variables (Tax, Association, Multiplex, Competition from other entertainment sectors and difficulty in obtaining government grants) of cine distributors of Kerala give **F values** of **15.921, 46.271, 48.584, 15.352 and 20.392** respectively, which are significant at 5 per cent level in all cases **(P<.05)**. This implies that there is difference in the mean scores obtained for Tax, Association, Multiplex, Competition from other entertainment sectors and Difficulty in obtaining government grants for the cine distributors across Kerala.

5.4 Methods Used for Promotion and Distribution of Films

5.4.1 Road Shows

A road show is one of the major promotional tools used by film distributors for the promotion of films. In this form of film distribution, the film is exhibited on a limited number of screens in big cities even before the actual release of the film on a large scale. This promotion tool is mainly adopted to create a demand for the film among the audience. Also, this technique helps to understand how the film is accepted by the audience and to make modifications, if needed,before the film is distributed on a large scale.

5.4.2 Discussions in Media

Another promotion tool used by distributors is media discussions. Nowadays various entertainment programs are started by various channels for discussing the latest movie updates in the industry. The discussions in such type of programs are another major platform used by distributors for promotion. Sakalakala, Puthen padam, Censor, Theatres ee varam etc; are some of the prominent television programs that help in the promotion of films by using the media in the industry.

5.4.3 Creative Banners

These are also outdoor advertising structures found in high-traffic areas. These are mainly displayed to attract the audience on a larger scale. Posters are mainly designed by experts in the field, who are appointed by the producer in consultation with the director. These designs are distributed to the distributors for movie promotion. Nowadays flex types of posters are gaining demand in the market due to the cheap cost and limited time consumption.

5.4.4 Internet Blogs

Internet blogs are another major promotional tool used by distributors nowadays. It comprises mainly discussion platform and informational websites. In this website, the most recent updates about the movies distributed by the distributor are posted, which include posters, pre-release videos, songs, promotion made by producers and actors, etc. Also the comments and suggestions of the audience about the movie are also made here. These blogs are maintained with the help of a computer professional in the field.

5.4.5 Hoardings

Hoardings are large outdoor advertising structures found mainly in high traffic areas. These are mainly displayed to attract the audience on a larger scale. One of the most common forms of hoardings is posters. Poster designs aremainly designed by an expert in the field, who is appointed by the producer in consultation with director. These designs are distributed to the distributors for movie promotion. Nowadays flex types of posters are gaining demand in the market due to the cheap cost and limited time consumption.

5.4.6 *Creative Banners*

These are also outdoor advertising structures found in high-traffic areas. These are mainly displayed to attract the audience on a larger scale. Posters are mainly designed by an expert in the field, who is appointed by the producer in consultation with director. These designs are distributed to the distributors for movie promotion. Nowadays flex types of posters are gaining demand in the market due to the cheap cost and limited time consumption.

5.4.7 *Partnerships*

Partnership is marketing cooperation with one or two companies or products. Here, the film advertisements are displayed in the company'sproduct or products for a specified period. Usually, products with high quality, brand image and heavy demand are selected for this purpose by the distributors. The movie logos, colour schemes, names of the movie, the director, the producer, the distributor,are usually displayed in the products. The main objective is to combine the strength of the brand with the film for the purpose of promotion. The movie distributors as well as the product manufacturers gain advantage by adopting this strategy.

5.4.8 *Events*

Events promotion tool simply involves a face-to-face contact between the audience and the distributor in various fairs, sporting events, etc. Here, the distributor uses techniques such as free sample tickets, tickets with discount vouchers, etc. These promotion tools help to build a lasting and powerful brand for the movie in the minds of the audience. The events can also be various conferences, seminars, trade shows, etc. The ultimate aim of the event is to educate the audience about the movie distributed.

5.4.9 *Guerilla Marketing*

Guerilla Marketing is one of the most prominent promotion tools having immense demand for distributors nowadays. This is an advertisement strategy designed by the distributor with or without the producer to promote a film with a very low budget. The major investment for creating this promotion tool is high imagination skill, energy and time. This promotion strategy is focused on creating a huge impression about the movie among the audience. For example, creating and circulating a video intentionally about the movie and maximizing its circulation. Some of the variants in guerilla marketing are viral and buzz marketing. The following Table shows the mean rank of the ıesponses ofSelected Cine Distributors towards the Major promotional tools

Table 5.21 Friedman Test-Mean Ranks

Elements	*Mean Rank*
Road Shows	**2.97**
Discussions in Media	3.41
Internet Blogs	3.68
Hoardings	5.56
Creative Banners	4.39
Partnerships	5.00
Events	5.45
Guerilla Marketing	5.54

(Source: Primary data)

Table 5.21 presents the mean ranks obtained for the eight tools used for promoting and distributing movies. The lower the mean ranks, the higher will be the preference, as rank one should have the lowest mean. Thus, from the Table it is evident that the element 'Road show' is the most important tool for promotion and distribution of movies (Mean rank= 2.97), followed by Discussion in media and Internet blogs with mean ranks of 3.41 and 3.68 respectively. Also, the least important tool that is used for promoting movies is Hoardings.

Table 5.22 Test Statistics[a]

N	310
Chi-Square	401.109
Df	7
Asymp. Sig.	*.000**

a. Friedman Test

*Significant at 5 per cent level

(Source: Primary data)

The Chi-square statistic provides a value of 401.109 which is significant at 5 per cent level. It may be concluded that there is significant variation in the preferences associated with the eight tools for promotion and distribution of movies.The following Table shows the mean ranks of the responses ofSelected Cine Distributors towards the major promotional tools

Table 5.23 Kruskal-Wallis Test -Mean Ranks

	Concentration in Film Distribution	*N*	*Mean Rank*
Road Shows	Malayalam	128	171.25
	Hindi	96	**120.67**
	Tamil	86	170.94
	Total	310	
Discussion in Media	Malayalam	128	195.25
	Hindi	96	**79.00**
	Tamil	86	181.73
	Total	310	

Internet Blogs	Malayalam	128	181.88
	Hindi	96	**58.67**
	Tamil	86	224.34
	Total	310	
Hoardings	Malayalam	128	145.88
	Hindi	96	**130.67**
	Tamil	86	197.55
	Total	310	
Creative Banners	Malayalam	128	146.00
	Hindi	96	215.50
	Tamil	86	**102.66**
	Total	310	
Partnerships	Malayalam	128	164.75
	Hindi	96	200.00
	Tamil	86	**92.06**
	Total	310	
Events	Malayalam	128	157.75
	Hindi	96	200.00
	Tamil	86	**102.48**
	Total	310	
Guerilla Marketing	Malayalam	128	170.13
	Hindi	96	164.33
	Tamil	86	**123.87**
	Total	310	

(Source: Primary data)

Table 5.24 Test Statistics[a,b]

	Road shows	Discussion in Media	Internet Blogs	Hoardings	Creative Banners	Partnerships	Events	Guerilla Marketing
Chi-Square	22.383	121.372	133.363	30.824	81.620	79.237	62.634	16.522
Df	2	2	2	2	2	2	2	2
Asymp. Sig.	.000*	.000*	.000*	.000*	.000*	.000*	.000*	.000*

a. Kruskal Wallis Test

b. Grouping Varicble: Concentration in filmexhibition

*Significant at 5 per cent level

(Source: Primary data)

From the above Tables, it is evident that 'Road show' is the most effective promotion methodfor film distributors concentrating in Hindi movies (Mean rank 120.67), followed by film distributors concentrating in Tamil and Malayalam movies with mean ranks 170.94 and 171.25 respectively. The lowest rank score indicates the highest preference.The Chi square value (22.383) is found to be significant at 5 per cent level. This indicates that there is significant difference in the preference of selected cine distributors associated with the 'Road show' method of promotion and distribution of Malayalam films.

Another promotion method 'Discussion in Media' is the most apt promotion tool for film distributors concentrating in Hindi movies (Mean rank 79.00), followed byfilm distributors concentrating in Tamil movies and Malayalam movies with mean ranks 181.73 and 195.25 respectively. The Chi-square value (121.372) is found to be significant at 5 per cent level. This indicates that there is significant difference in the preference of selected cine distributors associated with discussion in media for promotion and distribution of Malayalam films.

'Internet Blogs', another promotion tool, is the most suited for the promotion of distributors concentrating in Hindi movies (Mean rank 58.67). But this promotion tool is most unsuitable for film distributors concentrating in Tamil movies with mean rank 224.34. The Chi-square value (183.365) is found to be significant at 5 per cent level. This indicates that there is significant difference in the preference of selected cine distributors associated with Internet blog element of promotion and distribution of Malayalam films.

Another promotion tool, 'Hoardings' is the most suited for distributors concentrating in Hindi movies (Mean rank 130.67). But this promotion tool is most unsuitable for film distributors concentrating in Tamil movies with mean rank 197.55. The Chi-square value (30.824) is found to be significant at 5 per cent level. This indicates that there is significant difference in the preference of selected cine distributors associated with the Hoarding method of promotion and distribution of Malayalam films.

'Creative Banners' is the most suited for the distributors concentrating in Tamil movies (Mean rank 102.66). But this promotion tool is most unsuitable for film distributors concentrating in Hindi movies with mean rank 215.50. The Chi-square value (81.620) is found to be significant at 5 per cent level. This indicates that there is significant difference in the preference of selected cine distributors associated with 'Creative Banners' for promotion and distribution of Malayalam films.

'Partnerships' are the most suited for distributors concentrating in Tamil movies (Mean rank 92.06), followed by distributors concentrating in Malayalam and Hindi movies. The Chi-square value (79.237) is found to be significant at 5 per cent level. This indicates that there is significant difference in the preference of selected cine distributors associated with thepartnershipmethod for promotion and distribution of Malayalam films.

'Events' are the most suited for the promotion of films distributors concentrating in Tamil movies (Mean rank 102.48), followed by distributors concentrating in Malayalam and Hindi movies with mean ranks 157.75 and 200.00 respectively. The Chi-square value (62.634) is found to be significant at 5 per cent level. This indicates that there is significant difference in the preference of selected cine distributors associated with events for promotion and distribution of Malayalam films.

'Guerilla Marketing' is the most suited for the promotion of films for distributors concentrating in Tamil movies (Mean rank 123.87), followed by distributors concentrating in Hindi and Malayalam movies. The Chi-square value (16.522) is found to be significant at 5 per cent level. This indicates that there is significant difference in the preference of selected cine distributors associated with 'Guerilla Marketing' for promotion and distribution of Malayalam films.

So, it can be concluded that promotional methods such as Creative Banners, Partnerships, Events and Guerilla Marketing are most suitable for the promotion of films for distributors concentrating in Tamil movies, and promotional tools such as Road Shows, Discussion in Media, Internet Blogs and Hoardings are most suitable for the promotion of films for distributors concentrating in Hindi movies.The Following Table Shows the Mean Ranks of the Responses of Selected Cine Distributors towards the Major Promotional Methods.

Table 5.25 Kruskal-Wallis Test-Mean Ranks

	Experience in Film Distribution	*N*	*Mean Rank*
Road Shows	11-15 Years	61	**47.00**
	16-20 Years	153	214.65
	Above 20 Years	96	130.17
	Total	310	

Discussion in Media	11-15 Years	61	**79.00**
	16-20 Years	153	181.82
	Above 20 Years	96	162.17
	Total	310	
Internet Blogs	11-15 Years	61	**111.00**
	16-20 Years	153	164.98
	Above 20 Years	96	168.67
	Total	310	
Hoardings	11-15 Years	61	**63.00**
	16-20 Years	153	200.85
	Above 20 Years	96	142.00
	Total	310	
Creative Banners	11-15 Years	61	184.00
	16-20 Years	153	**138.59**
	Above 20 Years	96	164.33
	Total	310	
Partnerships	11-15 Years	61	150.43
	16-20 Years	153	**109.84**
	Above 20 Years	96	231.50
	Total	310	
Events	11-15 Years	61	200.00
	16-20 Years	153	**109.84**
	Above 20 Years	96	200.00
	Total	310	
Guerilla Marketing	11-15 Years	61	248.00
	16-20 Years	153	**80.35**
	Above 20 Years	96	216.50
	Total	310	

(Source: Primary data)

Table 5.26 Test Statistics[a,b]

	Road Shows	Discussion in Media	Internet Blogs	Hoardings	Creative Banners	Partnerships	Events	Guerilla Marketing
Chi-Square	174.442	68.883	19.849	118.003		126.719	91.217	238.242
Df	2	2	2	2	2	2	2	2
Asymp. Sig.	.000*	.000*	.000*	.000*	.001*	.000*	.000*	.000*

a. Kruskal Wallis Test

b. Grouping Variable: Experience in Film Distribution

**Significant at 5 per cent level*

(Source: Primary data)

Tables 5.25 and 5.26, it is evident that 'Road Show' is the most effective promotion tool for film distributors, having an experience in film distribution ranging from 11–15 years (Mean rank 47). The lowest rank score indicates the highest preference. The Chi-square value (174.442) is found to be significant at 5 per cent level. This indicates that there is significant difference in the preference of selected cine distributors associated with the Road Show way of promotion and distribution of Malayalam films.

Another promotion tool, 'Discussion in Media', is the most apt promotion tool for film distributors having an experience in film distribution ranging from 11 – 15 years (Mean rank 79), followed by film distributors having an experience in film distribution of above 20 years and 16-20 years with mean ranks 162.17 and 181.82 respectively.The Chi-square value (68.883) is found to be significant at 5 per cent level. This indicates that there is significant difference in the preference of selected cine distributors associated with discussion in media element of promotion and distribution of Malayalam films.

'Internet Blogs', another promotion tool, is the most suited for film distributors having an experience in film distribution ranging from 11-15 years (Mean rank 111). But this promotion tool is the most unsuitablefor film distributors having more than 20 years of distribution experience. Here, the Chi-square value (19.849) is found to be significant at 5 per cent level. This indicates that there is significant difference in the preference of selected cine distributors associated with the internet Blog element of promotion and distribution of Malayalam films.

Another promotion tool, 'Hoardings' is the most suited for film distributors having an experience in film distribution ranging from 11-15 years (Mean rank 63), followed by film distributors having an experience in film distribution of above 20 years and 16-20 years with mean ranks 142 and 200.85 respectively. The Chi-square value (118.003) is found to be significant at 5 per cent level. This indicates that there is significant difference in the preference of selected cine distributors associated with the 'Hoarding' element of promotion and distribution of Malayalam films.

'Creative Banners' is the most apt promotion tool for distributors having an experience in film distribution ranging from 16-20 years (Mean rank 138.59). But this promotion tool is the most unsuited for film distributors having a distribution experience of 11-15 years.The Chi-square value (13.770) is found to be significant at 5 per cent level. This indicates that there is significant difference in the preference of selected cine distributors associated with the 'Creative Banners' element of promotion and distribution of Malayalam films.

'Partnerships' are the most suited promotion tool for distributors having an experience in film distribution ranging from 16-20 years (Mean rank 109.84). The Chi-square value (126.719) is found to be significant at 5 per cent level. This indicates that there is significant difference in the preference of selected cine distributors associated with the 'Partnership' element of promotion and distribution of Malayalam films.

The 'Events' promotional tool is the most suited for distributors having an experience in film distribution ranging from 16-20 years with a mean rank of 109.84. The Chi-square value (91.217) is found to be significant at 5 per cent level. This indicates that there is significant difference in the preference of selected cine distributors associated with 'Event' element of promotion and distribution of Malayalam films.

'Guerilla Marketing' is the most suited promotion tool for distributors having an experience in film distribution ranging from 16-20 years (Mean rank 80.35). But this promotion tool is most unsuited for film distributors having a distribution experience of 11-15 years. The Chi-square value (238.242) is found to be significant at 5 per cent level. This indicates that there is significant difference in the preference of selected cine distributors associated with 'Guerilla Marketing' element of promotion and distribution of Malayalam films.

So, it can be concluded that promotional tools such as Creative Banners, Partnerships, Events and Guerilla Marketing are most suitable for the promotion of films of distributors having an experience in distribution ranging between 16 – 20 years, and that promotional tools such as Road Shows, Discussion in Media, Internet Blogs and Hoardings are suitable for the promotion of films of distributors having an experience in distribution ranging between 11– 15 years. The Following Table Shows the Mean Rank of the Responses of Selected Cine Distributors towards the Major Promotional Methods.

Table 5.27 Kruskal-Wallis Test - Mean Ranks

	Type of Film Distributed	*N*	*Mean Rank*
Road Shows	Adventure	153	**104.33**
	Comedy	93	228.49
	Crime	32	109.50
	Epics/Historical	32	234.00
	Total	310	
Discussion in Media	Adventure	153	**107.37**
	Comedy	93	201.48
	Crime	32	173.50
	Musical / Dance	32	234.00
	Total	310	
Internet Blogs	Adventure	153	**125.88**
	Comedy	93	175.33
	Crime	32	173.50
	Epics/Historical	32	221.50
	Total	310	
Hoardings	Adventure	153	**142.61**
	Comedy	93	158.82
	Crime	32	157.50
	Musical / Dance	32	205.50
	Total	310	
Creative Banners	Adventure	153	175.67
	Comedy	93	123.00
	Crime	32	**30.50**
	Epics/Historical	32	278.50
	Total	310	

Partnerships	Adventure	153	146.29
	Comedy	93	**107.52**
	Crime	32	200.00
	Epics/Historical	32	294.50
	Total	310	
Events	Adventure	153	157.45
	Comedy	93	**121.67**
	Crime	32	200.00
	Epics/Historical	32	200.00
	Total	310	
Guerilla Marketing	Adventure	153	186.63
	Comedy	93	**73.15**
	Crime	32	248.00
	Epics/Historical	32	153.50
	Total	310	

(Source: Primary data)

Table 5.28 Test Statistics[a,b]

	Road Shows	Discussion in Media	Internet Blogs	Hoardings	Creative Banners	Partnerships	Events	Guerilla Marketing
Chi-Square	154.001	111.855	42.091	14.725	156.426	131.593	35.852	143.383
Df	3	3	3	3	3	3	3	3
Asymp. Sig.	.000*	.000*	.000*	.002*	.000*	.000*	.000*	.000*

a. Kruskal Wallis Test

b. Grouping Variable: Type of Film Distributed by company

*Significant at 5 per cent level

(Source: Primary data)

Tables 5.27 and 5.28, it is evident that 'Road Shows' is the most effective promotion tool for film distributors concentrating in adventure type movies (Mean rank 104.33). The lowest rank score indicates the highest preference.The Friedman Chi-square value (154.001) is found to be significant at 5 per cent level. This indicates that there is significant difference in the preference of selected cine distributors associated with the 'Road Shows' element of promotion and distribution of Malayalam films.

'Discussion in Media' is the most apt promotion tool for film distributors concentrating in adventure type movies (Mean rank 107.37), followed by film distributors concentrating in crime type movies, and comedy type movies with mean ranks 173.50 and 201.48 respectively.The Friedman Chi-square value (111.855) is found to be significant at 5 per cent level. This indicates that there is significant difference in the preference of selected cine distributors associated with the'Discussion in Media' element of promotion and distribution of Malayalam films.

'Internet Blogs' is suited for film distributors concentrating in adventure type movies, havinga high mean rank of 125.88. But this promotion tool is most unsuitable for film distributors concentrating in epic/historical movies. The Friedman Chi-square value (42.091) is found to be significant at 5 per cent level. This indicates that there is significant difference in the preference of selected cine distributors associated with the 'Internet Blogs' element of promotion and distribution of Malayalam films.

'Hoardings' is most suited for film distributors concentrating in adventure type movies with mean rank 142.61. The Friedman Chi-square value (14.725) is found to be significant at 5 per cent level. This indicates that there is significant difference in the preference of selected cine distributors associated with the 'Hoarding' element of promotion and distribution of Malayalam films.

'Creative Banners' are aptfor film distributors concentrating incrime-oriented movies (Mean rank 30.50). But this promotion tool is most unsuited for film distributors concentrating in epic/historical movies. The Friedman Chi-square value (156.426) is found to be significant at 5 per cent level. This indicates that there is significant difference in the preference of selected cine distributors associated with the'Creative Banners' element of promotion and distribution of Malayalam films.

'Partnerships' are suited for distributors concentrating in comedy movies (Mean rank 107.52), followed by distributors concentrating in adventure movies, crime movies and historical movies. The Friedman Chi-square value (131.593) is found to be significant at 5 per cent level. This indicates that there is significant difference in the preference of selected cine distributors associated with the 'Partnerships' element of promotion and distribution of Malayalam films.

'Events' are most suited for distributors concentrating in comedy movies with mean rank 73.15. The Friedman Chi-square value (91.217) is found to be significant at 5 per cent level. This indicates that there is significant difference in the preference of selected cine distributors associated with the 'Events' element of promotion and distribution of Malayalam films.

'Guerilla Marketing' is suited for distributors concentrating in comedy movies with mean rank 73.15, followed by distributors concentrating in historical movies, adventure movies and crime movies. The Friedman Chi-square value (143.883) is found to be significant at 5 per cent level. This indicates that there is significant difference in the preference of selected cine distributors associated with the 'Guerilla Marketing' element of promotion and distribution of Malayalam films.

So, it can be concluded that promotional tools such as Road Shows, Discussion in Media, Internet Blogs and

Hoardings are most suited for the film distributors concentrating in adventure films. On the other hand, Partnerships, Events and Guerilla Marketing are apt promotion toolsfor distributors concentrating in comedymovies;for the distribution of crime movies, Creative Banners is the most suited promotion tool.

5.5 Conclusion

This chapter deals with the various marketing problems faced by film distributors in the Malayalam film industry. The important problems faced by distributors in the industry include increased tax rates, disputes arising between associations, competition from other segments of the entertainment sector, difficulty in obtaining of Government grants, etc. Even though various tools and techniques such as Road Shows, Discussions in Media, Internet Blogs, Hoardings and Creative Banners are used by distributors in-order to attract and increase audience response towards movies in theatres, the rise of DTH facilities and other sophisticated technologies has drastically reduced the demand for movies in theatres. By making use of statistical tools such as Kruskal Wallis test and Friedman test,it can berevealed that promotional tools such as Road Shows, Discussion in Media, Internet Blogs and Hoardings are most suitable for the promotion of adventure films; on the other hand, tools such as Partnerships, Events and Guerilla Marketing are best suited for distributors concentrating in comedy movies. The most effective tool for promotion and distribution of movies is 'Road Shows' followed by Discussion in Media and Internet Blogs; also the least effective toolused by distributors for promoting movies is 'Hoardings'.

REFERENCES

[1] Andy Field. (2010). *Discovering Statistics Using SAS Software,* 11-28.

[2] David Silverman (2010). *Quantitative Research,* Sage Publishers, 13-31.

[3] Erich Lechman., & George. (1998). *Theory of Point Estimation,* 11-22.

[4] Joseph Hair. (2010). *Multivariate Data Analysis,* Pearson Publication, 2-16.

[5] Kumar Pranab. (1986). *Contemporary Text Book on Statistical Analysis,* 480-549.

[6] Liese.,& Klaus. (2008). *Statistical Decision Theory,* 21-34.

[7] Mark J. (1987). *Review of Multivariate Analysis,* 391-411.

[8] Peter J. (2001). *Mathematical Statistics,* 16-38.

[9] Robert Torrie. (1977). *Principles and Procedures of Statistics,* 22-36.

[10] Stiglerr, Stephen M. (1978). *Mathematical Statistics in Early States,* 190-216.

[11] Wald, Abraham. (1947). *Sequential Analysis,* 18-57.

6

Problems of Cine Exhibitors in Kerala

The cine exhibitors functioning in the Malayalam film industry can be basically divided into three categories: they are A Class theatres, B Class Theatres and C Class theatres. All these exhibitors are facing enormous problems in the exhibition of films in their theatres. The problems faced by them may differ from theatre to theatre on the basis of class of theatre in which they are functioning, concentration of film exhibition in certain languages, experience in exhibition, type of films they are exhibiting, theatre owners' preference about the elements that attract the viewers, etc. The major marketing problems encountered by them include increased tax rates, advancement of piracy in the industry, difficulty in obtaining various grants from the Government, disputes that are arising between cine exhibitors' associations regarding various issues such as theatre cess percentages, ticket prices, etc. In addition to these problems, the various charges and fees imposed by Government authorities from time to time, difficulty in obtaining institutional funds from banks and other financial institutions for renovation and extension of theatres, etc, make the problems worse.

Here, inorder to study in depth about the marketing problems faced by cine exhibiters in the Malayalam film industry, 360 cine exhibitors are selected from a total population of 1156 by applying simple random sampling method. Out of the sample of 360, 180 cine exhibitors are from 'A class' theatres, 84 from 'B Class' theatres and 96 from 'C Class theatres'. Also, from the 360 samples selected, 51.9 per cent have an experience ranging from 16-20 years. A structured questionnaire is designed and distributed and data is collected from 360 selected cine exhibitors. Various problemsof exhibitors such as Piracy, Association, Tax, Ticket Prices, Sharing of profits, Class of Theatre, Digital RevolutionAdvancement, E-Ticketing, Theatre Cess Percentages, Promotion Problemof Cinemas, Difficulty in Obtaining of institutional funds and Government grants are taken into account inorder to study in detail about the marketing problems faced by the cine exhibitors in Malayalam movie industry.

Various statistical techniques such as Canonical Disciminant Analysis, Friedman Test, Kruskal Wallis Test, F Test, etc, are also being used in-order to understand in detail the level of these problems according to certain objects, how the problems are related to each other, and which class of exhibitors are more affected etc.

6.1 Frequency Distribution of the Cine Exhibitors Selected for the Study

Tables 6.1, 6.2 and 6.3 show the selected cine exhibitor's class of theatre owned, cine exhibitors' concentration in film exhibition and cine exhibitors' experience in exhibition.

Table 6.1 Class of Theatre Owned

	Frequency	*Percentage*	*Valid Percentage*	*Cumulative Percentage*
A Class	180	50.0	50.0	50.0
B Class	84	23.3	23.3	73.3
C Class	96	26.7	26.7	100.0
Total	360	100.0	100.0	

(Source: Primary data)

Table 6.2 Concentration of Film Exhibition

	Frequency	*Percentage*	*Valid Percentage*	*Cumulative Percentage*
Malayalam	134	37.2	37.2	37.2
Hindi	106	29.4	29.4	66.7
Tamil	120	33.3	33.3	100.0
Total	360	100.0	100.0	

(Source: Primary data)

Table 6.3 Experience in Film Exhibition

	Frequency	*Percentage*	*Valid Percentage*	*Cumulative Percentage*
11-15 Years	54	15.0	15.0	15.0
16-20 Years	187	51.9	51.9	66.9
Above 20	119	33.1	33.1	100.0
Total	360	100.0	100.0	

(Source: Primary data)

From Table 6.1, it is clear that 50 per cent of the selected cine exhibitors are functioning in A class, 23.3 per cent in B Class and 26.7 per cent in C class theatres. A majority of the cine exhibitors are functioning in A Class theatres.

By analyzing Table 6.2, it is observed that 37.2 per cent of the selected exhibitors functioning in the industry are concentrating more in the exhibition of Malayalam films, followed by Tamil and Hindi with a percentage of 33.3 and 29.4 respectively. So it is evident that the majority of the films exhibited in the industry are those in the Malayalam language.

From Table6.3, it is evident that, more than half the number (51.9) of the selected cine exhibitors functioning in the industry have an experience in film exhibition ranging from 16-20 years followed by those with above 20 years and 11-15 years of experience. So, we can conclude that the majority of the exhibitors functioning in the industry ahas 16-20 years of experience.

6.2 Marketing Problems of Cine Exhibitors

6.2.1 Tax

One of the major problems encountered by cine exhibitors in the industry is that of taxes. The taxes are imposed by the Central government, State government as well as the local bodies like municipalities and panchayaths. The Government levies tax in the form of sales tax, entertainment tax, multiplex tax, service tax, CBFC tax, etc. The rates of tax levied by these government bodies are also different. Another most important problem in tax is the frequent alterations made by the above-said government bodies, and the lack of awareness of cine exhibitors about the various tax shelters available under the law makes the situation more complicated. Unlike other foreign countries, the governments are not providing tax incentives to the various parties associated with the film exhibition which is also a great hindrance for the growth of the industry. The following Table shows the mean score of the responses of Selected Cine Exhibitors towards the Problem of Tax.

Table 6.4 Tests of Between-Subjects Effects

Dependent Variable: Tax

Source	*Type I Sum of Squares*	*Df*	*Mean Square*	*F*	*Sig.*
Class of theatre owned	190.633	2	95.317	10.325	***.000****
Concentration of Film Exhibition	21114.095	2	10557.048	1143.602	***.000****
Experience in film exhibition	1174.363	2	587.182	63.607	***.000****

Error	3258.684	353	9.231
Total	25737.775	359	

*Significant at 5 per cent level

(Source: Primary data)

Estimated Marginal Means

Table 6.5 Class of Theatre

Dependent Variable: Tax

Class of Theatre	*Mean*	*Std. Error*	*95% Confidence Interval*	
			Lower Bound	*Upper Bound*
A Class	**21.364**	.240	20.892	21.836
B Class	20.923	.348	20.238	21.607
C Class	19.876	.347	19.193	20.560

(Source: Primary data)

Table 6.6 Type of Film Concentration

Dependent Variable: Tax

Type of Film Concentration	*Mean*	*Std. Error*	*95% Confidence Interval*	
			Lower Bound	*Upper Bound*
Malayalam	**29.417**	.275	28.875	29.959
Hindi	10.800	.318	10.175	11.424
Tamil	21.947	.329	21.299	22.594

(Source: Primary data)

Table 6.7 Experience in Film Exhibition

Dependent Variable: Tax				
Experience in Film Exhibition	*Mean*	*Std. Error*	*95% Confidence Interval*	
			Lower Bound	*Upper Bound*
11-15 years	18.298	.460	17.393	19.203
16-20 years	20.275	.233	19.816	20.733
Above 20 years	**23.591**	.282	23.036	24.145

(Source : Primary data)

As per Tables 6.4, 6.5, 6.6 and 6.7, the problem of tax is found very high in A class theaters (Mean21.364), and cine exhibitors who concentrate on Malayalam films facethe difficulty of paying taxes (Mean 29.417). At the same time, considering the experience in exhibition, the exhibitors having more than 20 years of experience face this problem more seriously than other categories of exhibitors. The mean score variation is found significant at 5 percent level (P<.05) for all categories of cine exhibitors functioning in the industry.

6.2.2 *Association*

Another major problem encountered by cine exhibitors in the industry is the lack of coordination between the various cine exhibitors' associations. There is also the prevalence of various registered and unregistered cine exhibitors' associations functioning in the industry. The frequent conflicts arising between these associations are also of a great problem. Often number of associations prevents the release of certain movies in certain classes of theatres, which makes the problems worse; also, the difference in opinion across various associations regarding various issues is also of great concern to the industry. Even though the Government has formulated various policies in bringing the association problems to a minimum, the final results of these policies are not meeting the targeted objectives. The following Table shows the mean scores of the responses of selected Cine Exhibitors towards the problem of Association.

Table 6.8 Tests of Between-Subjects Effects

Dependent Variable: Association					
Source	*Type I Sum of Squares*	*Df*	*Mean Square*	*F*	*Sig.*
Class of Theatre	213.697	2	106.849	28.207	***.000****
Concentration of Film exhibition	10039.161	2	5019.580	1325.118	***.000****
Experience in film exhibition	458.944	2	229.472	60.578	***.000****
Error	1337.173	353	3.788		
Total	12048.975	359			

*Significant at 5 per cent level

(Source: Primary data)

Estimated Marginal Means

Table 6.9 Class of Theatre

Dependent Variable: Association				
Class of Theatre	*Mean*	*Std. Error*	*95% Confidence Interval*	
			Lower Bound	*Upper Bound*
A Class	13.332	.154	13.029	13.634
B Class	13.276	.223	12.838	13.714
C Class	11.698	.223	11.260	12.135

(Source: Primary data)

Table 6.10 Type of film concentration

Dependent Variable: Association				
Concentration in Exhibition	*Mean*	*Std. Error*	*95% Confidence Interval*	
			Lower Bound	*Upper Bound*
Malayalam	18.495	.176	18.148	18.842
Hindi	5.703	.203	5.303	6.103
Tamil	14.107	.211	13.693	14.522

(Source: Primary data)

Table 6.11 Experience in Exhibition

Dependent Variable: Association				
Experience in Exhibition	*Mean*	*Std. Error*	*95% Confidence Interval*	
			Lower Bound	*Upper Bound*
11-15 years	11.098	.295	10.518	11.678
16-20 years	12.643	.149	12.349	12.937
Above 20 years	**14.564**	.181	14.209	14.919

(Source: Primary data)

Tables 6.8, 6.9, 6.10 and 6.11 indicate that the problem of Association is very high in A class theatres (Mean 13.332), and the problem is very high in Malayalam film industry (Mean 18.495). At the same time, considering the experience the exhibitors having above 20 years of experience face the problem more seriously than other categories of exhibitors in the industry. The mean score is found significant at 5 percent level ($P<.05$) for all categories of cine exhibitors.

6.2.3 Multiplexes

Another major problem encountered by cine exhibitors in the industry is the concentration of film producers in multiplex release. Only a limited number of multiplexes are functioning in the industry, anda huge majority of the audience is attracted towards them. Even though huge ticket prices are charged from the audience in the multiplexes, and there is a great difference of tax in the release of movies in multiplexes, when compared to local theatres, the multiplex owners are able to fill the hall before the commencement of shows. Lack of infrastructure provided and bankruptcy of a majority of theatres functioning in the industry also boost the demand for multiplex releases. Increased acceptance of visual effects in films by the audience and DTH facilities provided by the multiplexes also increase the demand very rapidly. The following Table shows the mean score of the responses of Selected Cine Exhibitors towards the problem of Multiplex.

Table 6.12 Tests of Between-Subjects Effects

Dependent Variable: Multiplex

Source	*Type I Sum of Squares*	*Df*	*Mean Square*	*F*	*Sig.*
Class of Theatre	328.014	2	164.007	21.857	***.000****
Concentration of Film exhibition	15863.719	2	7931.859	1057.086	***.000****
Experience in film exhibition	1001.525	2	500.763	66.737	***.000****
Error	2648.742	353	7.504		
Total	19842.000	359			

*Significant at 5 per cent level

(Source: Primary data)

Estimated Marginal Means

Table 6.13 Class of Theatre

Dependent Variable: Multiplex				
Class of Theatre	*Mean*	*Std. Error*	*95% Confidence Interval*	
			Lower Bound	*Upper Bound*
A Class	**19.366**	.216	18.940	19.791
B Class	18.030	.314	17.413	18.647
C Class	17.314	.313	16.698	17.930

(Source: Primary data)

Table 6.14 Type of Film Concentration

Dependent Variable: Multiplex				
Type of Film Concentration	*Mean*	*Std. Error*	*95% Confidence Interval*	
			Lower Bound	*Upper Bound*
Malayalam	**24.658**	.248	24.170	25.147
Hindi	9.239	.286	8.675	9.802
Tamil	20.812	.297	20.229	21.396

(Source: Primary data)

Table 6.15 Experience in Exhibition

Dependent Variable: Multiplex				
Experience in Exhibition	*Mean*	*Std. Error*	*95% Confidence Interval*	
			Lower Bound	*Upper Bound*
11-15 years	18.552	.415	17.736	19.368
16-20 years	16.210	.210	15.796	16.623
Above 20 years	**19.948**	.254	19.448	20.447

(Source: Primary data)

As per Tables 6.12, 6.13, 6.14 and 6.15, it is clear that the problem of multiplex is found very high in A class theatres (Mean 19.366), and that the exhibitors who concentrate on Malayalam film industry are facing much difficulty (Mean 24.658). With regard to multiplexes, exhibitors having more than 20 years of experience in film exhibition have more problem with regard to multiplexes (Mean 19.948). The mean score variation is found significant at 5 percent level ($P<.05$) for all categories of cine exhibitors.

6.2.4 *Piracy*

One of the most vital problems encountered by cine exhibitors in the industry is Piracy. The absence of strict rules and regulations on the part of the Central government as well as State government has increased Piracy rapidly in the industry. Lack of coordination between producers' and cine exhibitors'associations in curbing Piracy is another major problem. Lack of knowledge on the part of cine exhibitors and producers in identifying and destroying the devices and sites for uploading movies makes the piracy issue more complicated. Statistics shows that there is a drastic demand for the pirated version movies in the society. The truth is that if everyone pirates the movies then no creative work can get done in the industry. The most effective method is to make the law very strict inorder to curtail this problem. The following Table shows the mean scores of the responses of Selected Cine Exhibitors towards the problem of Piracy.

Table 6.16 Tests of Between-Subjects Effects

Dependent Variable: Piracy					
Source	*Type I Sum of Squares*	*Df*	*Mean Square*	*F*	*Sig.*
Class of Theatre	908.892	2	454.446	34.441	*.000**
Type of Film Concentration	33018.719	2	16509.360	1251.190	*.000**

Experience in Exhibition	1815.201	2	907.600	68.784	***.000****
Error	4657.810	353	13.195		
Total	40400.622	359			

*Significant at 5 per cent level

(Source: Primary data)

Estimated Marginal Means

Table 6.17 Class of Theatre

Dependent Variable: Piracy

Class of Theatre	*Mean*	*Std. Error*	*95% Confidence Interval*	
			Lower Bound	*Upper Bound*
A Class	**28.162**	.287	27.598	28.726
B Class	28.012	.416	27.194	28.830
C Class	26.077	.415	25.260	26.894

(Source: Primary data)

Table 6.18 Type of Film Concentration

Dependent Variable: Piracy

Type of Film Concentration	*Mean*	*Std. Error*	*95% Confidence Interval*	
			Lower Bound	*Upper Bound*
Malayalam	**38.503**	.329	37.855	39.150
Hindi	15.775	.380	15.028	16.522
Tamil	27.973	.394	27.199	28.747

(Source: Primary data)

Table 6.19 Experience in Exhibition

Dependent Variable: Piracy				
Experience in Exhibition	*Mean*	*Std. Error*	*95% Confidence Interval*	
			Lower Bound	*Upper Bound*
11-15 years	28.001	.550	26.918	29.083
16-20 years	24.626	.279	24.078	25.174
Above 20 years	**29.624**	.337	28.961	30.287

(Source: Primary data)

It is observed from Tables 6.16, 6.17, 6.18 and 6.19 that the problem of Piracy has much affected A class theatres (Mean 28.162), and that exhibitors who concentrate on Malayalam film industry are much affected by this problem (Mean 38.503). But considering the experience of film exhibitors in exhibition, Piracy has much affected exhibitors having more than 20 years of experience (Mean 29.624). The mean score variation is found significant at 5 percent level ($P<.05$) for all categories of cine exhibitors.

6.2.5 Ticket Prices

One of the major problems encountered by cine exhibitors in the industry is the increased ticket prices. After the implementation of Goods and Services Tax (GST), there has been a huge hike in ticket prices compared to earlier days. The State Government implements GST in the form of SGST (State Government Service Tax) and the Central Government in the form of Central Government Service Tax (CGST). Both tax impositions and the frequent alterations made by Government bodies in tax structure have made exhibition a costly affair. Unlike other foreign countries, the Governments are not providing tax incentives to the various cine exhibitors functioning in the industry which also makes the situation worse. The following Table shows the mean scores of the responses of Selected Cine Exhibitors towards the problem of Ticket Prices.

Table 6.20 Tests of Between-Subjects Effects

Dependent Variable: Ticket Prices					
Source	*Type I Sum of Squares*	*Df*	*Mean Square*	*F*	*Sig.*
Class of Theatre	572.747	2	286.374	37.098	***.000****
Type of Film Concentration	10814.704	2	5407.352	700.499	***.000****
Experience in Exhibition	503.417	2	251.708	32.608	***.000****
Error	2724.906	353	7.719		
Total	14615.775	359			

*Significant at 5 per cent level

(Source: Primary data)

Estimated Marginal Means

Table 6.21 Class of Theatre

Dependent Variable: Ticket Prices				
Class of Theatre	*Mean*	*Std. Error*	*95% Confidence Interval*	
			Lower Bound	*Upper Bound*
A class	19.550	.220	19.118	19.982
B Class	**19.837**	.318	19.212	20.463
C Class	18.142	.318	17.517	18.766

(Source: Primary data)

Table 6.22 Type of Film Concentration

Dependent Variable: Ticket Prices

Type of Film Concentration	*Mean*	*Std. Error*	*95% Confidence Interval*	
			Lower Bound	*Upper Bound*
Malayalam	**25.817**	.252	25.322	26.312
Hindi	12.968	.290	12.397	13.539
Tamil	18.744	.301	18.152	19.336

(Source: Primary data)

Table 6.23 Experience in Exhibition

Dependent Variable: Ticket Prices

Experience in Exhibition	*Mean*	*Std. Error*	*95% Confidence Interval*	
			Lower Bound	*Upper Bound*
11-15 years	**20.427**	.421	19.599	21.255
16-20 years	17.463	.213	17.044	17.882
Above 20	19.638	.258	19.132	20.145

(Source: Primary data)

From Tables 6.20, 6.21, 6.22 and 6.23, it is clear that the problem of ticket prices has much affected B class theatres (Mean 19.837), followed by A class and C Class theatres with mean scores of 19.550 and 18.142 respectively. But, considering the concentration in film exhibition, the problem of ticket prices has much affected Malayalam movies (Mean 25.817). The ticket prices problem has much affected exhibitors having an experience ranging between 11-15 years (Mean 20.427). The mean score variation is found significant at 5 percent level ($P < .05$) for all categories of cine exhibitors.

6.2.6 Sharing of Profit

Another major problem encountered by cine exhibitors in the industry is the sharing of profits. The huge tax rate difference in sharing of profits on the basis of class of theatres owned by the cine exhibitors has made the situation more complicated. Also, there is no basic criterion on which the profit percentage is to be distributed to the producers of movies. Even though records such as Daily Collection Record (DCR) are there, the majority of the producers in the industry have the opinion that these records are manipulated by the exhibitors, showing lower income to the theatres in-order to reduce the profit share to the producers of the movies. In addition to it, after the introduction of the Goods and Services Tax (GST), the ticket prices also have drastically increased, which reduces the share of profit to the Cine Exhibitors in the Malayalam industry. The following Table shows the mean scores of the responses of Selected Cine Exhibitors towards the problem of Sharing of Profit.

Table 6.24 Tests of Between-Subjects Effects

Dependent Variable: Sharing of Profits

Source	*Type I Sum of Squares*	*Df*	*Mean Square*	*F*	*Sig.*
Class of Theatre	414.712	2	207.356	80.680	***.000****
Concentration in film exhibition	5273.082	2	2636.541	1025.857	***.000****
Experience in exhibition	210.922	2	105.461	41.034	***.000****
Error	907.240	353	2.570		
Total	6805.956	359			

*Significant at 5 per cent level

(Source: Primary data)

Estimated Marginal Means

Table 6.25 Class of Theatre

Dependent Variable: Sharing of Profits

Class of Theatre	*Mean*	*Std. Error*	*95% Confidence Interval*	
			Lower Bound	*Upper Bound*
A Class	14.681	.127	14.432	14.930
B Class	**14.822**	.184	14.460	15.183
C Class	13.411	.183	13.050	13.771

(Source: Primary data)

Table 6.26 Type of Film Concentration

Dependent Variable: Sharing of Profits

Concentration in Exhibition	*Mean*	*Std. Error*	*95% Confidence Interval*	
			Lower Bound	*Upper Bound*
Malayalam	19.074	.145	18.788	19.360
Hindi	10.182	.168	9.853	10.512
Tamil	13.657	.174	13.316	13.999

(Source: Primary data)

Table 6.27 Experience in Exhibition

Dependent Variable: Sharing of Profits

Experience in Exhibition	*Mean*	*Std. Error*	*95% Confidence Interval*	
			Lower Bound	*Upper Bound*
11-15 years	**15.564**	.243	15.087	16.042
16-20 years	13.222	.123	12.980	13.463
Above 20 years	14.127	.149	13.835	14.420

(Source: Primary data)

Tables 6.24, 6.25, 6.26 and 6.27 depict that the problem of sharing of profits has much affected B class theatres (Mean 14.822), followed by A class and C Class theatres with mean scores of 14.681 and 13.411 respectively. But, considering the concentration in film exhibition, the problem of ticket prices has much affected Malayalam movies (Mean score 19.074). The ticket prices problem has much affected exhibitors having an experience of 11-15 years (Mean 15.564). The mean score variation is found significant at 5 percent level ($P<.05$) for all categories of cine exhibitors.

6.2.7 *Class of Theatre*

Another major problem encountered by cine exhibitors in the industry is with regard to the class of theatre. The huge tax rate as well as the difference in sharing of profits on the basis of class of theatres owned by the cine exhibitors, is one of the major concerns. Also, the absence of a basic criterion on which the theatres should be divided into A Class, B Class and C Class theatres, is making the situation more complicated. In addition to that, conflicts are arising in the industry due to the non-release of certain movies by certain producers and distributors in certain classes of theatres, making the situation worse. In addition to that, the tax and other rates are determined on the basis of class of theatre in which the exhibitor is functioning which is another major problem. The following Table shows the mean scores of the responses of Selected Cine Exhibitors towards the problem of Class of Theatre.

Table 6.28 Tests of Between-Subjects Effects

Dependent Variable: Class of Theatre

Source	*Type I Sum of Squares*	*Df*	*Mean Square*	*F*	*Sig.*
Class of Theatre	547.547	2	273.774	91.363	***.000****
Concentration in film exhibition	7827.638	2	3913.819	1306.116	***.000****

Experience in exhibition	355.014	2	177.507	59.237	*.000**
Error	1057.776	353	2.997		
Total	9787.975	359			

*Significant at 5 per cent level

(Source : Primary data)

Estimated Marginal Means

Table 6.29 Class of Theatre

Dependent Variable: Class of Theatre

Class of Theatre	*Mean*	*Std. Error*	*95% Confidence Interval*	
			Lower Bound	*Upper Bound*
A Class	**19.659**	.137	19.390	19.928
B Class	18.474	.198	18.084	18.863
C Class	17.117	.198	16.728	17.506

(Source: Primary data)

Table 6.30 Type of Film Concentration

Dependent Variable: Class of Theatre

Type of Film Concentration	*Mean*	*Std. Error*	*95% Confidence Interval*	
			Lower Bound	*Upper Bound*
Malayalam	**24.373**	.157	24.065	24.682
Hindi	13.242	.181	12.886	13.597
Tamil	17.635	.188	17.266	18.004

(Source: Primary data)

Table 6.31 Experience in Exhibition

Dependent Variable: Class of Theatre				
Experience in Exhibition	*Mean*	*Std. Error*	*95% Confidence Interval*	
			Lower Bound	*Upper Bound*
11-15 Years	17.552	.262	17.037	18.068
16-20 Years	17.789	.133	17.528	18.050
Above 20 Years	**19.908**	.161	19.593	20.224

(Source: Primary data)

It is observed from Tables 6.28, 6.29, 6.30 and 6.31 that the problem of Class of Theatre has much affected A class theatres (Mean 19.659), followed by B class and C Class theatres with mean scores of 18.474 and 17.117 respectively. When considering the concentration in film exhibition, the problem of Class of Theatre is found to have much affected Malayalam movies (Mean 24.373). The problem of Class of Theatre has affected exhibitors having an experience of above 20 years (Mean 19.908). The mean score variation is found significant at 5 percent level (P<.05) for all categories of cine exhibitors.

6.2.8 Digital Revolution

Another major problem affecting the cine exhibiters is the advancement of digital technology. The traditional theatre owners find it very difficult to compete with the advanced technologies available at the new generation theatres and multiplexes in the industry. The vast visual effects and modern technologies available in the market are being unexplored by traditional owners. One of the major advancements in the digital revolution is the Dedicated to Sound (DTS) system which has a major impact on the growth of the industry. Also, other language movies exhibited in the theatres may be rich in visual effects, which leads to the non-acceptance of Malayalam movies in theatres. The following table shows the mean score of the responses of Selected Cine Exhibitors towards the problem of Digital Revolution.

Table 6.32 Tests of Between-Subjects Effects

Dependent Variable: Digital Revolution

Source	*Type I Sum of Squares*	*Df*	*Mean Square*	*F*	*Sig.*
Class of Theatre	666.731	2	333.366	53.138	***.000****
Type of Film Concentration	11050.460	2	5525.230	880.716	***.000****
Experience in Exhibition	350.104	2	175.052	27.903	***.000****
Error	2214.569	353	6.274		
Total	14281.864	359			

*Significant at 5 per cent level

(Source: Primary data)

Estimated Marginal Means

Table 6.33 Class of Theatre

Dependent Variable: Digital Revolution

Class of Theatre	*Mean*	*Std. Error*	*95% Confidence Interval*	
			Lower Bound	*Upper Bound*
A Class	19.022	.198	18.633	19.411
B Class	**19.518**	.287	18.953	20.082
C Class	16.982	.286	16.419	17.545

(Source: Primary data)

Table 6.34 Type of Film Concentration

Dependent Variable: Digital Revolution

Type of Film Concentration	*Mean*	*Std. Error*	*95% Confidence Interval*	
			Lower Bound	*Upper Bound*
Malayalam	**25.368**	.227	24.922	25.815
Hindi	11.996	.262	11.481	12.511
Tamil	18.157	.271	17.623	18.691

(Source: Primary data)

Table 6.35 Experience in Exhibition

Dependent Variable: Digital Revolution

Experience in Exhibition	*Mean*	*Std. Error*	*95% Confidence Interval*	
			Lower Bound	*Upper Bound*
11-15 Years	17.749	.379	17.003	18.495
16-20 Years	17.814	.192	17.436	18.192
Above 20 Years	**19.958**	.232	19.501	20.415

(Source: Primary data)

Tables 6.32, 6.33, 6.34 and 6.35 indicate that the problem of Digital Revolution has much affected B class theaters (Mean 19.518), followed by A class and C Class theatres with mean scores of 19.022 and 16.982 respectively. Considering the concentration in film exhibition, the problem of Digital Revolution is much found to have affected Malayalam movies (Mean 25.368). The problem of Digital Revolution has greatly affected exhibitors having an experience of above 20 years (Mean 19.958). The mean score variation is found significant at 5 percent level (P<.05) for all categories of cine exhibitors.

6.2.9 E-Ticketing

Another major advancement in the industry is Electronic Ticketing (E-Ticketing). The majority of the theatres in the industry are unaware of the vast electronic ticketing facilities available to the audience. Also, the huge service charges, in the form of State government service tax and Central government service tax has increased the electronic ticket prices to a much drastic level. Often the audience may complain that they are not getting seats in their preferred areas. The following Table shows the mean scores of the responses of Selected Cine Exhibitors towards the problem of E-Ticketing.

Table 6.36 Tests of Between-Subjects Effects

Dependent Variable: E-Ticketing

Source	*Type I Sum of Squares*	*Df*	*Mean Square*	*F*	*Sig.*
Class of Theatre	129.014	2	64.507	6.453	***.002****
Type of Film Concentration	12530.826	2	6265.413	626.805	***.000****
Experience in Exhibition	261.147	2	130.573	13.063	***.000****
Error	3528.513	353	9.996		
Total	16449.500	359			

*Significant at 5 per cent level

(Source: Primary data)

Estimated Marginal Means

Table 6.37 Class of Theatre

Dependent Variable: E-Ticketing				
Class of Theatre	*Mean*	*Std. Error*	*95% Confidence Interval*	
			Lower Bound	*Upper Bound*
A Class	18.231	.250	17.739	18.722
B Class	**18.284**	.362	17.571	18.996
C Class	17.790	.362	17.079	18.501

(Source: Primary data)

Table 6.38 Type of Film Concentration

Dependent Variable: E-Ticketing				
Type of Film Concentration	*Mean*	*Std. Error*	*95% Confidence Interval*	
			Lower Bound	*Upper Bound*
Malayalam	**24.733**	.287	24.169	25.297
Hindi	10.520	.331	9.870	11.170
Tamil	19.051	.343	18.378	19.725

(Source: Primary data)

Table 6.39 Experience in Exhibition

Dependent Variable: E-Ticketing				
Experience in Exhibition	*Mean*	*Std. Error*	*95% Confidence Interval*	
			Lower Bound	*Upper Bound*
11-15 Years	18.410	.479	17.468	19.352
16-20 Years	17.011	.243	16.534	17.488
Above 20 Years	**18.884**	.293	18.307	19.460

(Source: Primary data)

Tables 6.36, 6.37, 6.38, 6.39 depict that the problem ofE-Ticketing has much affected B class theatres (Mean 18.284), followed by A class and C Class theatres with mean scores of 18.231 and 17.790 respectively. Considering the concentration in film exhibition, the problem of E Ticketing has much affected Malayalam movies (Mean 24.773). The problem has severely affected exhibitors having an experience of above 20 years (Mean 18.884). The mean score variation is found significant at 5 percent level (P<.05) for all categories of cine exhibitors.

6.2.10 Theatre Cess Percentage

Another major problem encountered by cine exhibitors in the industry is with regard to theatre cess percentage, which leads to increase in ticket prices. The huge rate imposed by various authorities on the basis of class of theatres is one of the major concerns for the cine exhibitors in the industry. Also,the frequent alterations made in the cess percentage leads to certain conflicts among producers and exhibiters and local authorities. Often, certain additional fees and festival fees imposed by the authorities make the situation worse. In addition to this, the difference in rates of cess of multiplexes and theatres is also a major concern to the exhibitors. The following Table shows the mean scores of the responses of Selected Cine Exhibitors towards the problem of Theatre Cess Percentage.

Table 6.40 Tests of Between-Subjects Effects

Dependent Variable: Theatre Cess Percentage

Source	*Type I Sum of Squares*	*Df*	*Mean Square*	*F*	*Sig.*
Class of Theatre	160.222	2	80.111	3.319	*.037**
Type of Film Concentration	30570.229	2	15285.114	633.179	*.000**
Experience in Exhibition	108.224	2	54.112	2.242	.108
Error	8521.522	353	24.140		
Total	39360.197	359			

*Significant at 5 per cent level (Source: Primary data)

Estimated Marginal Means

Table 6.41 Class of Theatre

Dependent Variable: Theatre Cess Percentage				
Class of Theatre	*Mean*	*Std. Error*	*95% Confidence Interval*	
			Lower Bound	*Upper Bound*
A Class	27.477	.388	26.714	28.241
B Class	**28.088**	.563	26.982	29.195
C Class	27.564	.562	26.460	28.669

(Source: Primary data)

Table 6.42 Type of Film Concentration

Dependent Variable: Theatre Cess Percentage				
Type of Film Concentration	*Mean*	*Std. Error*	*95% Confidence Interval*	
			Lower Bound	*Upper Bound*
Malayalam	**37.316**	.445	36.440	38.192
Hindi	14.991	.514	13.980	16.001
Tamil	30.823	.532	29.776	31.870

(Source: Primary data)

Table 6.43 Experience in Exhibition

Dependent Variable: Theatre Cess Percentage				
Experience in Exhibition	*Mean*	*Std. Error*	*95% Confidence Interval*	
			Lower Bound	*Upper Bound*
11-15 Years	**28.821**	.744	27.358	30.285
16-20 Years	27.139	.377	26.398	27.881
Above 20	27.169	.456	26.273	28.066

(Source: Primary data)

Tables 6.40, 6.41, 6.42 and 6.43 depict that the problem of Theatre Cess Percentage has much affected B class theatres (Mean 28.088), followed by C class and A Class theatres with mean scores of 27.564 and 27.477 respectively. Considering the concentration in film exhibition, the problem of Theatre Cess percentage has much affected Malayalam movies (Mean 25.368). The problem of Theatre Cess percentage greatly affect exhibitors having an experience of 11-15 years (mean score 28.821). The mean score variation is found significant at 5 percent level according to class of theatre and type of film concentration (P<.05), but not significant to experience in film exhibition.

6.2.11 Promotion Problems

Another major problem encountered by cine exhibitors in the industry is the promotion problem. The theatre owner is often forced to adopt certain strategies due to the lack of promotion made by the producer of certain movies. But, the exhibitors will be less aware about the apt promotional strategies for the movies. The promotional strategies adopted by the cine exhibitors include 50 free tickets for first show, free family pass for families, etc. Lack of co-ordination and lack of adequate finance provided by producers for promoting movies are also matters of concern for the growth of the industry. The following Table shows the mean scores of the responses of Selected Cine Exhibitors towards the problem of Promotion.

Table 6.44 Tests of Between-Subjects Effects

Dependent Variable: Promotion Problem

Source	*Type I Sum of Squares*	*Df*	*Mean Square*	*F*	*Sig.*
Class of Theatre	568.214	2	284.107	17.938	***.000****
Type of Film Concentration	13506.351	2	6753.176	426.375	***.000****
Experience in Exhibition	87.916	2	43.958	2.775	.064

Error	5591.019	353	15.839
Total	19753.500	359	

*Significant at 5 per cent level

(Source: Primary data)

Estimated Marginal Means

Table 6.45 Class of Theatre

Dependent Variable: Promotion Problem				
Class of Theatre	*Mean*	*Std. Error*	*95% Confidence Interval*	
			Lower Bound	*Upper Bound*
A Class	22.320	.314	21.702	22.938
B Class	**25.258**	.456	24.361	26.154
C Class	23.252	.455	22.357	24.147

(Source: Primary data)

Table 6.46 Type of Film Concentration

Dependent Variable: Promotion Problem				
Type of Film Concentration	*Mean*	*Std. Error*	*95% Confidence Interval*	
			Lower Bound	*Upper Bound*
Malayalam	**29.789**	.361	29.080	30.499
Hindi	15.025	.416	14.206	15.843
Tamil	26.016	.431	25.168	26.864

(Source: Primary data).

Table 6.47 Experience in Exhibition

Dependent Variable: Promotion Problem				
Experience in Exhibition	*Mean*	*Std. Error*	*95% Confidence Interval*	
			Lower Bound	*Upper Bound*
11-15 Years	**24.602**	.603	23.416	25.787
16-20 Years	23.261	.305	22.661	23.862
Above 20 Years	22.967	.369	22.241	23.693

(Source: Primary data)

It is observed from Tables 6.44, 6.45, 6.46 and 6.47 that the problem of Promotion has much affected B class theatres (Mean 25.258), followed byC class and A Class theatres with mean scores of 23.252 and 22.320 respectively. Considering the concentration in film exhibition, the problem of promotion has affected the Malayalam movies more (mean 29.789). The problem of promotion has greatly affected exhibitors having an experience of 11-15 years (Mean 24.602). The mean score variation is found to be significant at 5 percent level ($P<.05$) according to class of theatre and type of film concentration, but the mean score variation is not significant in film exhibition since the P value is $>.05$.

6.2.12 Difficulty in Obtaining Government Grants

One of the major problems encountered by cine exhibitors is difficulty is the obtaining of government grants for the movies exhibited. The lack of financial support from State and Central governments in obtaining grants for theaters is a major hindrance to cine exhibiters functioning in the industry. Also, huge delays incurred in the sanctioning and distribution of these grants only among certain classes of theatres in the industry are also major problems affecting the industry. The presence of strict procedures in obtaining grants from the Government and difference in laws between Central and State governments in providing grants to theatres are also other hindrances in the obtaining of these grants. The following Table shows the mean scores of the responses of Selected Cine Exhibitors towards the Difficulty in the obtainment of Government Grants

Table 6.48 Tests of Between-Subjects Effects

Dependent Variable: Difficulty in Obtaining Government Grants

Source	*Type I Sum of Squares*	*Df*	*Mean Square*	*F*	*Sig.*
Class of Theatre	3286.220	2	1643.110	57.263	***.000****
Type of Film Concentration	29103.749	2	14551.875	507.140	***.000****
Experience in film exhibition	1235.387	2	617.693	21.527	***.000****
Error	10128.975	353	28.694		
Total	43754.331	359			

*Significant at 5 per cent level

(Source: Primary data)

Table 6.49 Class of Theatre

Dependent Variable: Difficulty in Obtaining Government Grants

Class of Theatre	*Mean*	*Std. Error*	*95% Confidence Interval*	
			Lower Bound	*Upper Bound*
A Class	37.033	.423	36.201	37.866
B Class	**40.996**	.613	39.789	42.202
C Class	34.673	.612	33.468	35.878

(Source: Primary data)

Table 6.50 Type of Film Concentration

Dependent Variable: Difficulty in Obtaining Government Grants

Type of Film Concentration	*Mean*	*Std. Error*	*95% Confidence Interval*	
			Lower Bound	*Upper Bound*
Malayalam	**47.493**	.486	46.538	48.448
Hindi	25.965	.560	24.864	27.066
Tamil	39.244	.580	38.102	40.385

(Source: Primary data)

Table 6.51 Experience in Exhibition

Dependent Variable: Difficulty in Obtaining Government Grants

Experience in Exhibition	*Mean*	*Std. Error*	*95% Confidence Interval*	
			Lower Bound	*Upper Bound*
11-15 Years	**41.015**	.811	39.419	42.611
16-20 Years	35.148	.411	34.339	35.956
Above 20 Years	36.540	.497	35.562	37.517

(Source: Primary data)

Tables 6.48, 6.49, 6.50 and 6.51 reveal that the difficulty in obtaining Government grants has much affected B class theatres (Mean 40.996), followed by A class and B Class theatres with mean scores of 37.003 and 34.673 respectively. Considering the concentration in film exhibition, the difficulty in obtaining Government grants has much affected Malayalam movies (Mean 47.493). The problem of obtaining Government grants has much affected exhibitors having an experience of 11-15 years (Mean 41.015). The mean score variation is found significant at

5 percent level (P<.05) for all categories of cine exhibitors in the industry.

6.2.13 Difficulty in the Obtaining of Institutional Fund

One of the major problems encountered by cine exhibitors in the industry is difficulty in the obtaining of Institutional Fund from banks and other financial institutions. There is a great hesitation on the part of the bank authorities in providing funds for revival of cinema theatres. Also, the cine-exhibiters find it very difficult for providing adequate assets as collateral security for loans,which makes the delay longer. The presence of strict procedures in obtaining funds from the banks and other Government agencies, and the lack of financial support from State and Central Governmentsare also great problems faced by the cine exhibiters in the industry. The following Table shows the mean scores of the responses of Selected Cine Exhibitors towards the Difficulty in the obtainment of Institutional Funds.

Table 6.52 Tests of Between-Subjects Effects

Dependent Variable: Difficulty in Obtaining Institutional Fund

Source	*Type I Sum of Squares*	*Df*	*Mean Square*	*F*	*Sig.*
Class of Theatre	2244.955	2	1122.478	52.687	***.000****
Type of Film Concentration	6669.338	2	3334.669	156.524	***.000****
Experience in film Exhibition	262.123	2	131.061	6.152	***.002****
Error	7520.515	353	21.305		
Total	16696.931	359			

*Significant at 5 per cent level

(Source: Primary data)

Estimated Marginal Means

Table 6.53 Class of Theatre

Dependent Variable: Difficulty in Obtaining Institutional Fund

Class of Theatre	*Mean*	*Std. Error*	*95% Confidence Interval*	
			Lower Bound	*Upper Bound*
A Class	22.262	.365	21.545	22.979
B Class	**24.998**	.529	23.959	26.038
C Class	18.825	.528	17.787	19.863

(Source: Primary data)

Table 6.54 Type of Film Concentration

Dependent Variable: Difficulty in Obtaining Institutional Fund

Type of Film Concentration	*Mean*	*Std. Error*	*95% Confidence Interval*	
			Lower Bound	*Upper Bound*
Malayalam	**26.312**	.418	25.489	27.135
Hindi	15.941	.483	14.992	16.890
Tamil	23.832	.500	22.849	24.816

(Source: Primary data)

Table 6.55 Experience in Exhibition

Dependent Variable: Difficulty in Obtaining Institutional Fund

Experience in Exhibition	*Mean*	*Std. Error*	*95% Confidence Interval*	
			Lower Bound	*Upper Bound*
11-15 Years	**23.665**	.699	22.290	25.040
16-20 Years	21.617	.354	20.920	22.313
Above 20 Years	20.804	.428	19.962	21.646

(Source: Primary data)

From Tables 6.52, 6.53, 6.54, and 6.55 it is clear that the difficulty in obtaining Institutional fund has much affected B class theatres (Mean 24.998), followed by A class and C Class theatres with Mean of 22.262 and 18.825 respectively. Considering the concentration in film exhibition, the difficulty in obtaining Institutional funds is found to have much affected in Malayalam movies (Mean 26.312). The problem of obtaining Institutional funds has much affected exhibitors having an experience of 11-15 years (Mean 23.665). The mean score variation is found significant at 5 percent level of significance ($P<.05$) for all categories of cine exhibitors in the industry.

6.3 Elements Attracting Viewers for Watching Films in Theatres

6.3.1 Story

One of the major elements that attract viewers for watching movies in theatres is the Story. A Story could be something which is an extension of plot with/without dialogues. It is normally brief in nature. When the story is expressed or modified by an expert in the field, taking into account camera angles, various shots, cuts, dialogues, expressions, camera movements etc., it becomes a screenplay. For developing a screenplay, enormous skill is required for the screenplay writer.These developed screenplays can be original works or adaptations from existing writing. In screenplays, the movements, actions, expressions, and dialogues of the characters are also narrated. The screenplay writer must be well aware about what is on the screen, and what is behind the screen. The experts in the field consider it as the backbone of films.

6.3.2 Star Cast

Another major factor that attracts viewers for watching movies in theatres is star cast. Casting refers to the process of selecting actors to play the various roles. Casting is just moulding the actor into a required character. Selections are done for finding the right actor to play the character in the film. A Casting Directors is a person authorized to do this work. He is responsible for matching the ideal actor to each role, based on a number of factors, such as the actor's experience, ability, reputation, availability, box office appeal, etc. He works both with the Director and the Producer to assemble the perfect cast for the film.Very often, the success or failure of the movies is dependent on the star cast. The final casting decisions are done by directors, in consultation with the story writer, the screenplay writer and the producer. Having a good star cast is a great boost to movie success.

6.3.3 *Music*

Another dominant element that attracts viewers for watching movies in theatres is music. The development of film music consists insong writing, film score also called background music, payment to singers, payment to music directors, other technicians, recording lab, etc. Depending on the nature of film, the film scores also change.The Music director is the key person who coordinates all the music-related activities in a film. He is also responsible for selecting the ideal singer for the song, in consultation with the director and the producer. Singer's experience, ability, reputation, availability, box office appeal, etc, also play a vital role in the selection of a singer. He works both with the Director and the Producer to assemble the perfect person for film music. Enormous movies in the industry had made huge success in box office only with the acceptance of film music by the public.

6.3.4 *Banner*

A major element that attracts audience for watching movies in theatres is the banner under which the film is produced. There are enormous film producers in the industry. When audience decide to watch movies in theatres they will look on the producer and banner under which the film is produced. Depending on the banner under which the movie is produced, the audience analyzes the previous movies produced under the banner and establishes an expectation inmind regarding the movie. Also, the advertisement used for the promotion of movies is dependent upon the banner under which the movie is made.

6.3.5 Advertisement

Another major element that attracts viewers for watching movies in theatres is advertisement. The success of a movie to a great extent depends on advertisement. The producers of movies spend enormous amounts towards advertisement. The advertisement methods used for promotion of films include road shows, discussion in media, internet blogs, hoardings, creative banners, creation of events, etc. All these types of advertisement techniques are used to promote the films in the audience market. Depending on the type of film and the class of audience for whom the film is made, the advertisement technique also changes. For example, if the movie is produced focusing children, the advertisement will be given in children's magazines or children's channels. Likewise if the movie is produced forthe teen-aged group, the advertisement will be in social networking channels like facebook, watsapp, etc.The following table shows the Mean Rank of the responses ofSelected Cine Exhibitors towards the Element of attraction by the Viewers.

Table 6.56 Friedman Test - Mean Ranks

Element	*Mean Rank*
Story	**2.35**
Star Cast	2.70

Music	2.84
Banner	3.54
Advertisement	3.57

(Source: Primary data)

Table 6.56, provides the mean ranks obtained for the five elements attracting audience for watching movies in theatres. The lower the mean ranks, the higher will be the preference, as rank one should have the lowest mean. Thus, from the Table it is evident that 'story' is the most important element that attracts the viewers in watching movies in theaters (Mean rank2.35), followed by star cast and music with mean ranks of 2.70 and 2.84 respectively. Also the least important element that attracts viewers is advertisement.

Table 6.57 Test Statistics (Friedman Test)

N	360
Chi-Square	167.069
Df	4
Asymp. Sig.	*.000**

*Significant at 5 per cent level

(Source: Primary data)

The Chi-Square statistic provides a value of 167.069 which is significant at 5 percent level (P<.05). It may be concluded that there is significant variation among the preferences associated with the five elements of attraction by viewers. The following table shows the Mean Rank of the responses ofSelected Cine Exhibitors towards the element (story) of attraction by the viewers.

Table 6.58 Kruskal-Wallis Test - Mean Ranks

	Class of Theatre	*N*	*Mean Rank*
Story	A Class	180	**161.80**
	B Class	84	198.64
	C Class	96	199.69
	Total	360	

(Source: Primary data)

Table 6.59 Test Statistics[a,b]

	Story
Chi-Square	13.575
Df	2
Asymp. Sig.	***.001****

a. Kruskal Wallis Test

b. Grouping Variable: Class of Theatre

*Significant at 5 per cent level

(Source: Primary data)

Kruskal-Wallis Test

Table 6.60 Mean Ranks

	Concentration in Exhibition	*N*	*Mean Rank*
Story	Malayalam	134	177.10
	Hindi	106	**148.90**
	Tamil	120	212.22
	Total	360	

(Source: Primary data)

Table 6.61 Test Statistics[a,b]

	Story
Chi-Square	24.591
Df	2
Asymp. Sig.	*.000**

a. Kruskal Wallis Test
b. Grouping Variable: Concentration in Exhibition
*Significant at 5 per cent level
(Source: Primary data)

Kruskal-Wallis Test

Table 6.62 Mean Ranks

	Experience in Exhibition	*N*	*Mean Rank*
Story	11-15 Years	54	**144.50**
	16-20 Years	187	209.68
	Above 20 Years	119	150.99
	Total	360	

(Source: Primary data)

Table 6.63 Test Statistics[a,b]

	Story
Chi-Square	35.875
Df	2
Asymp. Sig.	.000*

a. Kruskal Wallis Test
b. Grouping Variable: Experience in Exhibition
*Significant at 5 per cent level
(Source: Primary data)

From Table 6.58, it is evident that 'Story' is the most attractive element to the viewers in A Class theatres (Mean rank 161.80), followed by B and C class theatres with mean ranks 198.64 and 199.69 respectively.The lowest rank score indicates the highest preference. Also,while analyzing Table 6.62, the 'Story' is found to be the most attractive element to viewers of cine exhibition having an 11-15 years (Mean rank 144.50) of exhibition experience. Considering the concentration in exhibition, the element 'Story' is most attractive to the audience concentrating in Hindi movies (Mean rank 148.90), followed by exhibitors concentrating in Malayalam movies and Tamil movies with mean ranks of 177.10 and 212.22 respectively.

The Chi-square value is found to be significant at 5 percent level. This indicates that there is significant difference in the preference of selected cine exhibitors associated with the story element of attraction by the viewers. The following table shows the Mean Rank of the Responses ofSelected Cine Exhibitors towards the Element (Star Cast) ofAttraction by the Viewers

Table 6.64 Kruskal-Wallis Test - Mean Ranks

	Class of Theatre	*N*	*Mean Rank*
Star cast	A Class	180	**161.10**
	B Class	84	203.64
	C Class	96	196.63
	Total	360	

(Source: Primary data)

Table 6.65 Test Statistics[a,b]

	Star Cast
Chi-Square	15.135
Df	2
Asymp. Sig.	**.001***

a. Kruskal Wallis Test

b. Grouping Variable: Class of Theatre

*Significant at 5 per cent level

(Source: Primary data)

Table 6.66 Kruskal-Wallis Test - Mean Ranks

	Concentration of film exhibition	*N*	*Mean Rank*
Star Cast	Malayalam	134	**167.93**
	Hindi	106	168.28
	Tamil	120	205.33
	Total	360	

(Source: Primary data)

Table 6.67 Test Statistics[a,b]

	Star Cast
Chi-Square	12.202
Df	2
Asymp. Sig.	**.002***

a. Kruskal Wallis Test

b. Grouping Variable: Concentration of film exhibition

*Significant at 5 per cent level

(Source: Primary data)

While analyzing Tables 6.64, 6.65, 6.66 and 6.67, it is clear that the element of 'star cast' is the most attractive element to the viewers in A Class theatres (Mean rank 161.10), followed by C and B class theatres (Mean rank 196.63 and 203.64)respectively. The lowest rank score indicates the highest preference. Considering the concentration in exhibition, the element 'star cast' is the most attractive to the audience concentrating in Malayalam movies (Mean rank 167.93), followed by exhibitors concentrating in Hindi and Tamil movies. The Chi-square value is found to be significant at 5 percent level. This indicates that there is significant difference in the preference of selected cine exhibitors associated with the'star cast' element of attraction by the viewers.

6.4 The Most Dominant Problem Faced by Cine Exhibitors of Films inMalayalam and Other Languages

6.4.1 Tax

The most prominent issue encountered by cine exhibitors of film is Malayalam and other Indian languages is tax. The taxes are imposed by the Central and State Governments and also by local bodies like municipalities and corporations. The government levies taxes in the form of sales tax, entertainment tax, multiplex tax, service tax, Central Board of Film Certification tax, etc. The rates of tax levied by the various government bodies also differ. Also the frequent alterations made by the abovesaid Government bodies, and the lack of awareness of cine exhibitors about the various tax sheltersavailable under the law, are a great drawback to the industry.

6.4.2 Association

Another major issue faced by cine exhibitors concentrating in Malayalam and other language films is the lack of coordination between associations. There are a large number of conflicts and issues arising among the various registered and unregistered cine exhibitors' associations. The difference in opinion of various associations regarding various issues and non-release of certain movies in certain classes of theatres by the pressure of certain associations make the problems worse. Even though the changing governments have formulated various policies in bringing aboutcoordination between associations, a clear cut problem solving has not yet been done by any government agencies

6.4.3 Multiplex

Another major hindrance encountered in cine exhibition of films in Malayalam and other languages is the concentration of film producers in multiplex releases. Even though only a small number of multiplexes are functioning in the industry, a great percentage of the audiences are attracted towards them. So, the producers are also interested in multiplex release. The inability of theatre owners in providing good infrastructure, and the bankruptcy of a majority of theatres functioning in the industry are some of the reasons that increase the demand for multiplex releases. The visual effects environment and DTH facilities provided by the multiplexes are also another major reason for the increased demand.

6.4.4 Piracy

The most prominent issue encountered by cine exhibitors of films in Malayalam and other languages is piracy. The absence of strict rules and regulations on the part of the government has increased piracy to a great extent. The absence ofcoordination between producers', distributors' and cine exhibitors' associations in curbing piracy is also another major barrier. Recent studies by various government and NGO bodies show that there is an increased demand for the pirated version movies in the society. The best and most effective thing that can be done to curtail piracy is to make the law very strong.

6.4.5 Ticket Prices

Another major issue faced by cine exhibitors concentrating in Malayalam films and other language films is the increased ticket prices. The ticket price consists of show charge and other charges imposed by thegovernment from time to time. In recent times, ticket prices have showeda great hike due to the implementation of Goods and Services Tax (GST). The SGST (State Government Service Tax) and CGST (Central Government Service Tax) are the two major ingredients of GST tax. Also, the alterations made by government bodies in tax structure and problems regarding E-Ticketing have created a great headache to the exhibitors functioning in the industry.

6.4.6 Sharing of Profits

Another major hindrance encountered in cine exhibition of films in Malayalam and other languages is the sharing of profits. The absence of a basic criterion for how the profits must be divided makes the issue more complicated. The increased tax rate difference in the sharing of profits on the basis of class of theatres owned by the cine exhibitors has also created various issues in the industry. In addition to it, after the introduction of Goods and Services Taxthe cine exhibitors are of the opinion that theirshare of profit has reduced drastically compared to previous years.

6.4.7 Class of Theatre

One of the most prominent issues encountered by cine exhibitors of films in Malayalam and other languages is with regard to the class of theatre owned. The absence of a basic criterion on which the theatres should be divided into A Class, B Class and C Class, and the prevalence of a great tax rate difference in sharing of profits on the basis of class of theatres owned by the cine exhibitors, are the major concerns. Also the conflicts are arising in the industry due to the non release of certain movies by certain producers and distributors in certain classes of theatres which makes the situation worse.

6.4.8 Digital Revolution

Another major issue faced by cine exhibitors concentrating on films in Malayalam film and other languages is the advancement of digital technology. This problem has mainly affected the traditional theatre owners, who find it very difficult to compete with multiplexes using very advanced technologies available in the market. One of the major innovations which boosted the film industry is the introduction of Dedicated to Sound (DTS) systems. Also the lack of infrastructure for projecting the visual effects and increased competition from other language movies which are rich with visual effects,have also lead to the non-acceptance of Malayalam movies in Kerala theatres.

6.4.9 E – Ticketing

A major advancement in the industry is the system of Electronic Ticketing (E-Ticketing). A large percentage of the cine exhibitors in the industry are unaware of the vast electronic ticketing facilities available to the audience. Also the huge service charge in the form of State government service tax and Central government service tax has increased the electronic ticket prices to a much unaffordable level. Viewers often complain that they are not getting seats in their preferred areas. The increased time taken for loading the theatre sites for reservation is also a great problem.

6.4.10 Theatre Cess Percentage

One of the most common issues encountered by cine exhibitors of films in Malayalam and other languages is the theatre cess percentage. The huge tax and other rate imposed by various authorities on the basis of class of theatres are the major concerns for the cine exhibitors functioning in the industry. In addition to that the frequent changes made in the proportion ofcess percentage lead to variousconflicts between producers, exhibiters and the local authorities. Many a times certain additional fees and festival fees imposed by the authorities also cause great difficulties in film exhibition. The huge difference in the cess percentage of multiplexes and local theatres is also a major concern to the exhibitors.

6.4.11 Promotion Problem

A major problem encountered by cine exhibitors of films in Malayalam and other languages is the promotion problem. Owing to the lack of promotion made by the producers, the cine exhibitors are forced to adopt certain strategies. But the reality is that exhibitors may not be aware ofthe apt promotional strategies for the particular movie, which change in accordance with the nature of the film. Various promotional strategies are adopted by the cine exhibitors, including 50 free tickets for first show, free family pass for families, etc. Lack of coordination and lack of adequate finance from producers for promoting movies are also a hindrances to movie promotion.

6.4.12 Difficulty in obtaining Government Grants

One of the serious problems faced by cine exhibitors in Malayalam and other languages is the difficulty in obtaining government grants for movies exhibited. The lack of financial support from State and Central governments in the form of grants for theatres is a major hindrance to cine exhibiters functioning in the industry. The huge delay incurred in the sanctioning of grants, and distribution of these grants only among certain classes of theatres in the industry, are also major problems affecting the industry. There is the prevalence of strict procedures in obtaining grants from the government; also the huge difference in laws between Central and State governments in providing grants to theatres is also another hindrance in the obtainment of the grants.

6.4.13 Difficulty in the Obtaining of Institutional Fund

One of the major issues encountered by cine exhibitors in the Malayalam film industry is difficulty in the obtaining Institutional Funds from financial institutions. Nowadays, there seems to be a great hesitation on the part of the bank authorities in providing funds to cine exhibitors. The funds are borrowed for the revival of cinema theatres and for further expansions. The immense difficulty in providing adequate assets to financial institutions as collateral security against loans makes the delay longer. The stringent rules and procedures in obtaining funds from banks and other financial agencies, and the lack of financial support from the State and Central governmentsare also great hindrancesfaced by the cine exhibiters in the industry.

6.5 Discriminant Analysis – Malayalam / Other Languages

Here multiple discriminant analysis is used to identify the most critical problem that affects the cine exhibitors of Malayalam film industry concentrating in Malayalam and other languages. The output of multiple discriminant analysis is presented in the Tables 6.68, 6.69 and 6.70.

Table 6.68 Wilks' Lambda

Test of Function(s)	*Wilks' Lambda*	*Chi-square*	*Df*	*Sig.*
1	.087	858.699	13	*.000**

*Significant at 5 per cent level

(Source : Primary data)

Table 6.69 Functions at Group Centroids

Language	*Function* 1
Malayalam	4.198
Other Languages	-2.489

(Unstandardized canonical discriminant functions evaluated at group means)

Table 6.70 Standardized Canonical Discriminant Function Coefficients

	Function 1
Tax	-.570
Association	.576
Multiplex	-3.067
Piracy	3.457
Ticket Prices	-2.026
Sharing of Profit	1.945
Class of Theatre	.276
Digital Revolution	.980
E –Ticketing	-.256
Theatre Cess Percentage	.639
Promotion Problem	-.504
Difficulty in Obtaining Government Grant	-.118
Difficulty in Obtaining Institutional Fund	-.954

The Wilks Lambda Matirx (Table 6.68) of Discriminant Analysis gives a statistically significant Chi-square value (values of Chi-square **858.699 with p=000<.05**), which means that the discriminant function for identifying the most critical problem of cine exhibitors functioning in Malayalam film industry is valid.

From the function at group centroids (Table 6.69) negative coefficients are found for problems of cine exhibitors offilms in other languages and positive coefficients are foundfor the problems of cine exhibitors of Malayalam films. Therefore from the standardized canonical discriminant function coefficient matrix (Table 6.70), it can be observed that Piracy **(3.457)**, Sharing of Profit **(1.945)** and Digital Revolution **(.980)**, have the highest positive coefficients. Similarly Multiplex **(-3.067)** and Ticket Prices **(-2.026)** have the highest negative coefficients.

Therefore, as per the coefficients in the group centroid matrix and Standardized Canonical Discriminant Function matrix, it can be concluded that Piracy is the most vital problem faced by exhibitors of films in Malayalam language, followed by Sharing of Profit and Digital Revolution, whereas Multiplex is the most important problem faced by exhibitors of films in other languages, followed by Ticket Prices and Difficulty in Obtaining Institutional Funds.

6.6 Conclusion

This chapter deals with the various marketing problems faced by film exhibitors in the industry. The important problems faced by exhibitors in the industry include Increased Tax Rates, Disputes between Associations, Disputes on Issues such as Sharing of Profits, Rise in Ticket Prices, E-Ticketing Problems, Difficulty in Obtaining Government Grants and Institutional Funds, etc. By making use of the Canonical Discriminant Function Matrix, it is inferred that Piracy is the most vital problem faced by exhibitors of films in Malayalam language, followed by Sharing of Profit and Digital Revolution. On the other hand, Multiplex is the most important problem faced by cine exhibitors in other languages, followed by Ticket

Prices and Difficulty in Obtaining Institutional Funds. The Friedman test reveals that 'Story' is the most important element that attracts the viewers to watch movies in theaters, followed by Star Cast and Music. Also, the least important element that attracts the viewers to movies in theatres is Advertisement.

REFERENCES

[1] Andy Field. (2010). *Discovering Statistics Using SAS Software,* 11-28.

[2] David Silverman (2010). *Quantitative Research,* Sage Publishers, 13-31.

[3] Erich Lechman., & George. (1998). *Theory of Point Estimation,* 11-22.

[4] Joseph Hair. (2010). *Multivariate Data Analysis,* Pearson Publication, 2-16.

[5] Kumar Pranab. (1986). *Contemporary Text Book on Statistical Analysis,* 480-549.

[6] Liese., & Klaus. (2008). *Statistical Decision Theory,* 21-34.

[7] Mark J. (1987). *Review of Multivariate Analysis,* 391-411.

[8] Peter J. (2001). *Mathematical Statistics,* 16-38.

[9] Robert Torrie. (1977). *Principles and Procedures of Statistics,* 22-36.

[10] Stiglerr, Stephen M. (1978). *Mathematical Statistics in Early States,* 190-216.

[11] Wald, Abraham. (1947). *Sequential Analysis,* 18-57.

7

Summary of Findings, Conclusion and Recommendations

7.1 Introduction

The producers, distributors and cine exhibitors functioning in the Malayalam film industry are facing enormous problems. The problems faced by them may differ on the basis of the type of films produced, the type of ownership in the production company, the experience of film producers in the production field, the concentration of producers in certain language films, the class of theatre on which the distributors and cine exhibitors are focusing, the concentration of film exhibitors in certain languages, the experience of exhibitors in film exhibition etc.

The major problems encountered by them include increased tax rates, prevalence of piracy in the industry, difficulty in the obtaining of various grants from the government, disputes that are arising between various associations regarding issues such as theatre cess percentages, ticket prices, difficulty in obtainment of institutional funds from banks and other financial institutions for expanding their production and marketing channels.

The film industry was selected for the study because it is an unexplored area in research, and also to understand in-depth the production and the marketing problems faced in the Malayalam film industry. The film industry is a dominant sector in the economy. It plays a positive and important role in the overall development of the economy. The performance of the film sector has an indirect effect on the other industrial and service sectors functioning in the economy. The identification of the problems faced by film sector is also of great importance since the revenue generated by this sector towards the national income is very high. Thus a study on the **Production and Marketing Problems of Malayalam Film Industry** is considered to be highly relevant.

The main objectives of the study were to examine the various production and marketing problems faced by producers in Malayalam film industry, to analyze the various marketing problems faced by distributors and cine exhibitors in the industry, to identify the various marketing strategies adopted by the producers, distributors and cine exhibitors to tackle the various problems encountered by them, and also to make recommendations to the industry on the basis ofthe findings of the study.

The study is based on primary data. The primary data was collected from selected producers, distributors and cine exhibitors functioning in Malayalam film industry, using a pre-structured questionnaire. From the total producers' population of 113, 80 producers were selected by using Simple Random Sampling. Likewise, 310 distributors and 360 cine exhibitors were selected out of the total population of 904 and 1156 respectively. The design of the present study is descriptive and analytical in nature. The data collected from these three groups were edited, coded and analyzed, using Statistical Package for Social Sciences (SPSS Version 17). Statistical tools such as Friedman Test, Kruskal Wallis Test, ONE WAY–ANOVA, Canonical Disciminant Analysis, etc., were used for establishing and analyzing the dependence and relation between the variables considered.

7.2 Summary of Findings

The major findings of the study are reported below.

7.2.1 Demographic Profile of Producers, Distributors and Cine Exhibitors Selected for the Study

1) Among the 80 film producers selected for the purpose of this study, a large number (55 per cent) had single ownership in production house and 45 per cent hadpartnership ownership in production house. A majority of the film producers (62.5 per cent) were operating in production as well as in distribution. Further, 46.3 per cent of the selected film producers functioning in the industry had an experience in film production above 20 years, followed by producers' having 16-20 year experience and 11-15 years experience.

2) As many as 41.3 per cent of the selected distributors concentrated in the distribution of Malayalam movies, 31 per cent in the distribution of Hindi movie and 27.7 per cent in the distribution of Tamil movies.

3) With regard toexperience in distribution, 49.4 per cent of the film distributors had an experience ranging from 16-20 years, followed by distributors having experience of above 20 years and 11-15 years. When type of films distributed by thecompany was taken into account,a large majority of the distributors (49.4 per cent) were found to focus on adventure type movies, and only 10.3 per cent on crime and epic type movies.

4) Among the 360 cine Exhibitors selected for the study, 50 per cent were functioning in A class, 23.3

per cent in B Class and 26.7 per cent were functioning in C class theatres. Also,37.2 per cent of the selected exhibitors were concentrating more in the exhibition of Malayalam films, followed by Tamil and Hindi with a percentage of 33.3 and 29.4 respectively.

5) When experience of cine exhibitors was considered, 51.9 per cent of the selected cine exhibitors were found to have an experience in film exhibition ranging from 16-20 years, followed by those with more than 20 years of exhibition experience, and the rest with 11-15 years of exhibition experience.

7.2.2 Production Problems Faced by Producers in Malayalam film industry

1) With regard to the **Difficulty in the Obtaining of Government Grants** faced by the selected film producers in Malayalam film industry, the problem was found very high for Producers having a **partnership** ownershipin the production house (**Mean score 69.279**) and producers who concentrate on **production only** also faced this problem very seriously (**Mean score 53.934**). At the same time, considering the experience in production, producers having an experience of **11 – 15 years** faced this problem more seriously than other categories of producers.The mean score variation wasfound statistically significant at 5 per cent level (P<.05) for type of ownership in the production company and experience of producers in production.

2) In the case of **Cast and Crew**-related problems, the Producers having a **partnership** ownership in the production house (**Mean score 34.757**) and producers who concentrated on **production only** faced this problem more seriously (**Mean score 26.913**). At the same time, considering the experience in production, producers having an **experience of**

11 – 15 years faced this problem more seriously than the other categories of producers. Also, the mean score variation was found significant at 5 per cent level (P<.05) for all categories of film producers functioning in the industry.

3) With regard to the **Focus on Stardom** related problems, the film producers having a **partnership** ownership in the production house (**Mean score 46.160**) faced the problem seriously. At the same time, considering the experience of film producers in production, producers having an **experience of 11-15 years** faced the problem more seriously than other categories of producers in the industry. The mean score variation was found significant at 5 per cent level for all categories of film producers functioning in the industry.

4) When the problems relating to **Copyright and Intellectual Property Rights** were considered, the producers having a **partnership** ownership in the production house (**Mean score 46.631**) and producers who concentrated on **production only** faced this problem very seriously **(Mean score 45.522)**. At the same time, considering the experience in production, producers having an experience of **11 – 15 years** faced this problem more severely than other categories of producers. The mean score variation was also found significant at 5 per cent level (P<.05) for all categories of film producers functioning in the industry.

5) In the case of**Difficulty in Identification and Obtaining of Sources of Funds**-related problems, the Producers having a **partnership** ownership in the production house (**Mean score 48.201**) and producers who concentrated on **production only** faced this problem more seriously (**Mean score 38.859**). At the same time, considering the experience

in production, the producers having an experience of **11 – 15 years** faced this problem more seriously than other categories of producers functioning in the industry. The mean score variation was found significant at 5 per cent level (P<.05) for type of ownership in the production company and experience of producer in production, but not significant for producer's movie operation in the industry.

6) From the study, it was observed that the problem of **Visual Effects Industry** was very high for Producers having a **partnership** ownership in the production house (mean score **30.956**) and producers who concentrated on **production only** faced this problem very high (Mean score **25.951**). At the same time, considering the experience in production, the producers having an experience of **11 – 15 years** faced this problem more seriously than other categories of producers. The mean score variation was found significant at 5 per cent level (P<.05) for type of ownership in the production company and experience of producers in production.

7.2.3 Marketing Problems Faced by Producers Functioning in Malayalam Film Industry

1) It was observed from the study that the problem of **Piracy** greatly affected film producers having **partnership** ownership in the production houses (Mean score **57.042**). At the same time, considering the experience of film producers in production, the producers having an experience of **11-15 years** faced the problem more seriously than other categories of producers in the industry. Also, producers operating in **production and distribution** faced this problem the most. The mean score variation was found significant at 5 per cent level

(P<.05) for all categories of film producers functioning in the industry.

2) It was understood from the study that the problem of **Tax** very much affected producers havinga **partnership** ownership in the production houses (Mean score **45.190**). At the same time, considering the experience of film producers in production, producers having **above 20 years** of experience faced the problem more seriously than other categories of producers in the industry. Also, producers concentrating in **production and distribution** faced this problem the most. The mean score variation was found significant at 5 per cent level (P<.05) for all categories of film producers functioning in the industry.

3) With regard to **Central Board of Film Certification**-related problems the producers having a **partnership** ownership in production houses (Mean score **36.342**) faced this problem severely. At the same time, considering the experience of film producers in production, the producers having **above 20 years** of experience faced the problem more seriously than other categories of producers in the industry. Also, producers concentrating in **production and distribution** faced this problem more seriously. The mean score variation was found significant at 5 per cent level (P<.05) for type of ownership in the production company and experience of producers in production, but not significant for producers' movie operation in the industry.

4) **Multiplex**-related problems greatly affected film producers who had a **partnership** ownership in the production houses (Mean score **40.475**). At the same time, considering the experience of film producers in production, the producers having an

experience of **above 20 years** faced the problem more seriously than other categories of producers in the industry. The mean score variation was found significant at 5 per cent level of significance (P<.05) for type of ownership in the production company and experience of producer in production, but not significant for producers' movie operation in the industry.

5) From the analysis, it could be concluded that the problem of **Competition from Other Entertainment Sectors**much affected film producers having **partnership** ownership in the production houses (Mean score **34.440**). At the same time, considering the experience of film producers in production, the producers having an experience of **above 20 years** faced the problem more than other categories of producers in the industry. Also the producers operating in **production and distribution** faced this problem seriously. The mean score variation was found significant at 5 per cent level (P<.05) for type of ownership in the production company and experience of producer in production, but not significant for producers' movie operation in the industry.

6) As per the Coefficients in the Group Centroid Matrix and Standardized Canonical Discriminant Function Matrix, was concluded that **Difficulty in Identification and Obtaining of Sources of Fund** was the most critical problem faced by film producers having partnership ownership in companies followed by Cast and Crew and Difficulty in Obtaining Government Grants, whereas **Copyright and Intellectual Property Rights** was the most important problem faced by film producers having single ownership in companies, followed by Focus on Stardom and visual effects industry.

7) By analyzing the Coefficient in the Group Centroid Matrix and Standardized Canonical Discriminant Function Matrix, it could be concluded that **Difficulty in Identification and Obtaining of Sources of Fund** was the most vital problem faced by film producers operating in production and distribution, followed by Cast and Crew and Story, whereas **Copyright and Intellectual Property Rights** was the most important problem faced by film producers operating in production only, followed by difficulty in obtaining government grant and visual effects industry.

8) It was evident from the mean scoresof the responses of selected film producers on the **Difficulty in the Obtaining of Government Grants** that producers having more than 20 years of production experience and producers having production experience of 11-15 years faced the problem more seriously than other categories of producers in the industry. The highest mean scores were those of producers having above 20 years of production experience (**Mean score 46.7**) and 11-15 years experience (**Mean score 45.0**). The mean score variation was found not statistically significant at 5 per cent level **(Value of F = .127 with P = .881>.05)**. So, it would be concluded that there was no difference in the mean scores obtained for Government Grants related problems.

9) The Table also revealed that the mean scoresof responses of **Cast and Crew-** related problems were high for producers having an experience of **16-20 years** and **11-15 years**. The highest mean scores were those of producers having a production experience of 16-20 years **(Mean score 25.4),** followed by film producers having 11-15 years of experience. The mean score variation was not found statistically

significant at 5 per cent level **(value of F = 2.492 with P = .089>.05)**. So, it could be inferred that there was no difference in the mean scores obtained for Cast and Crew-related problems.

10) Producers having a production experience of **16-20 years** faced **Story**-related problems more seriously than any other category of producers. The highest mean scores were obtained for film producers having production experience of 16-20 years (**Mean score 29.7**) and above 20 years (**Mean score 12.3810**). The mean score variation was found statistically significant at 5 per cent level **(Value ofF = 4.773 with P=0.011<.05)**. Thus, it could be concluded that there was difference in the mean scores obtained for Story-related production problems.

11) Based on the mean scoresof the responses of selected film producers on **Focus on Stardom**-related problems, producers having production experience of 11-15 years and producers having above 20 years of production experience faced the problem seriously. The highest mean scores were those of producers having **11-15 years**of experience (**Mean score 63.0**) and producers having **16-20 years**of experience (**Mean score 30.7**). The mean score variation was found statistically significant at 5 per cent level (**Value of F = 45.802 with P = .000<.05**). So it could be concluded that there was difference in the mean scores obtained for focus on stardom-related problems.

12) This study revealed that **Copyright and Intellectual Property Rights**-related problems highly affectedproducers having production experience of **above 20 years** with **Mean score 33.1**,followed by film producers having production experience of **16-20 years** and **11-15 years**. The mean score variation was statistically significant at 5 per cent

level **(Value of F = 4.191 with P=0.019<.05)**. Thus, it could be concluded that there was difference in the mean scores obtained for Copyright and Intellectual Property Rights-related problems.

13) Considering the**Difficulty in Obtaining of Sources of Funds** producers having production experience of above 20 years faced more serious problems than any other category of film producers. The highest mean scores were those for producers having **above 20 years** of production experience (**Mean score 31.5**) and **11-15 year** production experience (**Mean score 30.0**). The mean score variation was found not statistically significant at 5 per cent level **(Value of F = .578 with P=0.564>.05)**, which implied that there was no difference in the mean scores obtained for the Difficulty in Obtaining of Sources of Funds related problems.

14) The mean scores of the responses on**Visual Effects Industry**-related problems revealed that the producers having an experience of 11-15 years and 16-20 years faced the problem seriously. The highest mean scores were those of producers having a production experience of **11-15 years(Mean score 20.0),** followed by film producers having **16-20 years**of experience. The mean score variation was not statistically significant at 5 per cent level **(Value of F = .062 with P = .940>.05)**. So it could be inferred that there was no difference in the mean scores obtained for visual effects industry-related problems.

15) Based on the mean scores of responses of selected film producers on **Piracy**-related problems, producers having production experience of 11-15 years and producers having production experience ranging between 16-20 years faced the problem more seriously than other categories of producers

in the industry. The highest mean sores were those of producers having **11-15 years** of production experience (**Mean score 45.0**) and **16-20 year** experience (**Mean score 44.2**). Also, the mean score variation was not statistically significant at 5 per cent level **(Value of F= .271 with P = .763>.05)**. So, it could be concluded that there was no difference in the mean scores obtained for Piracy related problems.

16) **Tax** related problems highly affectedproducers having production experience of **above 20 years** with a **mean score of 42.9,** followed by film producers having production experience of **16-20 years** and **11-15 years**. The mean score variation was statistically significant at 5 per cent level **(Value ofF = 13.187 with P=0.000<.05)**. Thus it could be concluded that there was difference in the mean scores obtained for Tax-related problems.

17) Regarding **Central Board of Film Certification**-related problems, producers having production experience of above 20 years faced more serious problems than any other category of film producers. The highest mean scoreswere those for producers having **above 20 years** of production experience (**Mean score 30.5**) and **16-20 years**of production experience (**Mean score 28.5**). The mean score variation was not statistically significant at 5 per cent level **(Value of F = 2.461 with P=0.092>.05)**, which implied that there was no difference in the mean scores obtained for Central Board of Film Certification related problems.

18) The **Multiplexes**-related problems highly affected producers having production experience of **above 20 years** with a**mean score of 32.4,** followed by film producers having production experience of **16-20 years** and **11-15 years**. The mean score

variation was not statistically significant at 5 per cent level **(Value ofF = 1.901 with P=.156>.05)**. Thus, it could thus be concluded that there was no difference in the mean scores obtained for Multiplex-related problems.

19) With regard to **Competition from Other Entertainment Sectors** related problems, producers with an experience of above 20 years and 16-20 years were found to face problemsvery seriously. The highest mean scores were those of producers having a production experience of **above 20 years (Mean score 29.1),** followed by film producers having **16-20 years** of experience. The mean score variation was not statistically significant at 5 per cent level **(Value of F = .954 with P = .390>.05).** So, it could be inferred that there was no difference in the mean scores obtained for Cast and Crew-related problems.

7.2.4 Marketing Problems Faced by Cine Distributors Functioning in Malayalam Film Industry

1) It was understood from the study that the problem of **Tax**was very high for distributors concentrating in **Malayalam Movies (Mean 41.696)**.Considering the experience in distribution, the distributors having an experience of **11-15 years** faced this problem more seriously than distributors having an experience of **16-20 years** and **above 20 years**. The mean score variation was found significant at 5 per cent level (P<.05) for all categories of cine distributors functioning in the industry.

2) Considering the **Association** problems faced by film distributors in the industry, distributors who were concentrating more in **Malayalam Movies (Mean score 43.059)** faced the problem more seriously. At the same time distributors having an

experience of **16-20 years** faced the problem more seriously than other categories of distributors in the industry. The mean score variation was found significant at 5 per cent level according to concentration in film distribution (P<.05), but not significant for experience in film distribution (P>.05).

3) It was clear from the study that the problem of **Multiplex** was very high in **A class theatres** (**Mean score 19.366**), and the distributors who concentrated in **Malayalam film industry**were facing much difficulty (**Mean score 24.658**). With regard to multiplexes, exhibitors having more than **20 years** of experience in film exhibition had great problem with regard to multiplexes (**Mean score 19.948**). The mean score variation was found significant at 5 per cent level (P<.05) for all categories of cine distributors.

4) From the study it could be concluded that **Competition from Other Entertainment Sectors** affected the functioning of distributors who were concentrating more in **Malayalam movies** (**Mean score 33.917**), followed by Tamil movies and Hindi movies with mean scores 30.760 and 16.167 respectively. Considering the experience in film distribution, distributors having a distribution experience of **11-15 years** faced the problem more seriously than other categories of distributors in the industry. The mean score variation was found significant at 5 per cent level (P<.05) for all categories of cine distributors.

5) The results of **One-Way ANOVA** for the variables (Tax, Association, Multiplex, Competition from other entertainment sectors, and Difficulty in obtaining government grants) revealed that cine distributors of Kerala gave **F values** of **15.921, 46.271, 48.584, 15.352 and 20.392** respectively, which was significant

at 5 per cent level in all cases **(P<.05)**. This implies that there was difference in the mean scores obtained for Tax, Association, Multiplex, Competition from other entertainment sectors and Difficulty in obtaining government grants for the cine distributors across Kerala.

6) The Kruskal-Wallis Test revealed that promotional tools such as **Creative Banners, Partnerships, Events and Guerilla Marketing** were the most suitable for the promotion of films distributors concentrating in Tamil movies, and promotional tools such as **Road Shows, Discussion in Media, Internet Blogs and Hoardings**for the promotion of film distributors concentrating in Hindi movies.

7) It was also found that promotional tools such as **Creative Banners, Partnerships, Events and Guerilla Marketing** were most suitable for the promotion of films of distributors having an experience in distribution ranging between **16 – 20 years,** and that promotional tools such as **Road Shows, Discussion in Media, Internet Blogs and Hoardings** were suitable for the promotion of films of distributors having an experience in distribution ranging between **11– 15 years**.

8) From the study, it could be found that promotional tools such as **Road Shows, Discussion in Media, Internet Blogs and Hoardings** were most suited for the film distributors concentrating in **adventure films**. On the other hand, **Partnerships, Events and Guerilla Marketing** were apt promotion tools for distributors concentrating in **comedy movies,** and that for the distribution of crime movies, **Creative Banners** were the best suited promotion tool.

7.2.5 Marketing Problems Faced by Cine Exhibitors in Malayalam film Industry

1) It could be understood that the problem of **Tax**was very high in **A class theatres (Mean score 21.364)** and cine exhibitors who concentrated in **Malayalam films** faced the difficulty of paying tax (**Mean score 29.417**). At the same time, considering the experience in exhibition, the exhibitors having **more than 20 years of experience** faced this problem more seriously than other categories of exhibitors. The mean score variation was found significant at 5 per cent level (P<.05) for all categories of cine exhibitors functioning in the industry.
2) From the study it was understood that the problem of **Association** was very high in A **class theatres (Mean score 13.332)**, and that the problem was very high in the **Malayalam film industry** (**Mean score 18.495**). At the same time, the exhibitors having **above 20 years of experience** faced the problem more seriously than other categories of exhibitors in the industry. The mean score was found significant at 5 per cent level (P<.05) for all categories of cine exhibitors.
3) It was clear from the study that the problem of **Multiplex**was very high in **A class theatres (Mean score 19.366)**, and that exhibitors who concentrated on **Malayalam films** were facing much difficulty (**Mean score 24.658**). With regard to multiplexes, exhibitors having **more than 20 years of experience** in film exhibition had much problem with regard to multiplexes (**Mean score 19.948**). The mean score variation was found significant at 5 per cent level of significance (P<.05) for all categories of cine exhibitors.

4) It was observed that the problem of **Piracy** much affected**A class theatres (Mean score 28.162)**, and the exhibitors who concentrate on Malayalam film industry were much affected by this problem (**Mean score 38.503**). But, considering the experience of film exhibitors in exhibition, Piracy greatly affected exhibitors having **more than 20 years of experience (Mean score 29.624**). The mean score variation was found significant at 5 per cent level (P<.05) for all categories of cine exhibitors.

5) The studyrevealed that the problem of **Ticket Prices**greatly affected**B class theatres (Mean score 19.837)**, followed by A class and C Class theatres with mean scores of 19.550 and 18.142 respectively. But, considering the concentration in film exhibition, the problem of ticket prices severely affected **Malayalam movies (Mean score 25.817)**. The ticket prices problem greatly affected exhibitors having an experience of**11-15 years (Mean score 20.427)**. The mean score variation was found significant at 5 per cent level (P<.05) for all categories of cine exhibitors.

6) The study depicted that the problem of Sharing of profits greatly affected **B class theatres (Mean score 14.822)**, followed by A class and C Class theatres with mean scores of 14.681 and 13.411 respectively. But, considering the concentration in film exhibition, the problem of ticket prices had much affected **Malayalam movies (Mean score 19.074)**. The ticket prices problem severely affected exhibitors having an experience of**11-15 years (Mean score 15.564)**. The mean score variation was found significant at 5 per cent level (P<.05) for all categories of cine exhibitors.

7) It was observed that the problem of Class of Theatre affected **A class theatres** very much **(Mean score**

19.659), followed by B class and C Class theatres with mean scores of 18.474 and 17.117 respectively. Considering the concentration in film exhibition, the problem of Class of theatre greatly affected **Malayalam movies (Mean score 24.373)**. The problem Class of Theatre greatly affected exhibitors having an **experience of above 20 years** (**Mean score 19.908**). The mean score variation was found significant at 5 per cent level (P<.05) for all categories of cine exhibitors.

8) The study indicated that the problem of **Digital Revolution** affected **B class theatres (Mean score 19.518)** much, followed by A class and C Class theatres with mean scores of 19.022 and 16.982 respectively. Considering the concentration in film exhibition, the problem of Digital Revolution much affected **Malayalam movies (Mean score 25.368)**. The problem of Digital Revolution greatly affected exhibitors having an **experience above 20 years (Mean score 19.958)**. The mean score variation was found significant at 5 per cent level (P<.05) for all categories of cine exhibitors.

9) The study revealed that the problem of **E-Ticketing** had much affected **B class theatres (Mean score 18.284)**, followed by A class and C Class theatres with mean scores of 18.231 and 17.790 respectively. Considering the concentration in film exhibition, the problem of E Ticketing is much affected in **Malayalam movies (Mean score 24.773)**. The problem had much affected exhibitors having an **experience of above 20 years (Mean score 18.884)**. The mean score variation was found significant at 5 per cent level (P<.05) for all categories of cine exhibitors.

10) From the study it became clear that the problem of **Theatre Cess Percentage** severely affected **B**

class theaters (Mean score 28.088), followed by C class and A Class theatres with mean scores of 27.564 and 27.477 respectively. Considering the concentration in film exhibition, the problem of theatre cess percentage much affected **Malayalam movies (Mean score 25.368)**. The mean score variation was found significant at 5 per cent level according to class of theatre and type of film concentration (P<.05), but not significant for experience in film exhibition.

11) It was be observed that the problem of Promotion is greatly affected**B class theatres (Mean score 25.258)**, followed by C class and A Class theaters with mean scores of 23.252 and 22.320 respectively. Considering the concentration in film exhibition, the problem of Promotion much affected **Malayalam movies (Mean score 29.789)**. The problem of Promotion greatly affected exhibitors having an **experience of11-15 years (Mean score 24.602)**. The mean score variation was found to be significant at 5 per cent level (P<.05) according to class of theatre and type of film concentration, but the mean score variation was not significant for experience in film exhibition since the P valuewas >.05.

12) It could be understood that the **Difficulty in Obtaining Government Grants** much affected **B class theatres** very much **(Mean score 40.996)**, followed by A class and B Class theaters with mean scores of 37.003 and 34.673 respectively. Based on the concentration in film exhibition the difficulty in obtaining Government Grants had much affected **Malayalam movies (Mean score 47.493)**. The problem of obtaining Government grants greatly affected exhibitors having an experience of **11-15 year (Mean score 41.015)**. The mean score variation

was found significant at 5 per cent level (P<.05) for all categories of cine exhibitors in the industry.

13) The study revealed that the **Difficulty in Obtaining Institutional Funds** is greatly affected **B class theatres (Mean score 24.998)**, followed by A class and C Class theaters with mean scores of 22.262 and 18.825 respectively. Based on the concentration in film exhibition the difficulty in obtaining of Institutional funds was found to have much affected **Malayalam movies (Mean score 26.312)**. The problem of obtaining Institutional fundsgreatly affected exhibitors having an experience of **11-15 years (Mean score 23.665)**. The mean score variation was found significant at 5 per cent level (P<.05) for all categories of cine exhibitors in the industry.

14) It was found out that the element,**Story** was the most important one that attracted the viewers to movies in theaters, followed by **Star Cast and Music**. Also, the least important element that attracted the viewers to movies in theatres was **Advertisement**.

15) It could be concluded that **Piracy** was the most vital problem faced by cine exhibitors in Malayalam language, followed by **Sharing of Profit and Digital Revolution**, whereas **Multiplex** was the most important problem faced by cine exhibitors in other languages, followed by **Ticket prices and Difficulty in Obtaining Institutional Funds**.

7.3 Testing of Hypotheses

1) There is no difference in the production problems faced by producers who run firms independently or on a partnership basis

This hypothesis was tested by applying Multiple

discriminant analysis and the output showed that there was significant difference in the production problems faced by such producers. The null hypothesis was rejected, as the Wilk's Lambda indicated by the Chi-square was found statistically significant at 5 per cent level (value of Chi-square = 121.999 with P = .000<.05)

2) There is no difference in the production problems faced by producers who concentrate on Production only / Production and distribution.

Multiple discriminant analysis was applied to test the null hypothesis and it could be seen that the Wilk's Lambda indicated by the chi-square is found statistically significant at 5 per cent level (value of Chi-square = 171.399 with P = .000<.05). So, the null hypothesis was rejected, with a conclusion that the production problems were different for those producers who concentrated on production only and those who concentrated on production and distribution.

3) There is no difference in the methods used by Cine Exhibitors to attract the audience to theatres in Malayalam film industry.

Friedman test was applied to test the null hypothesis and it was found that the value of Friedman Chi-square was significant at 5 per cent level (value of Chi-square = 167.069 with P = .000<.05). Therefore, the null hypothesis was rejected with a conclusion that the elements for attracting the viewers to theatres in Malayalam film industry were different.

4) There is no difference in the preference of audience about the story of films exhibited by different classes of theatres in Malayalam film industry.

The Kruskal-Wallis test was applied to test the null hypothesis and the output showed that the value of Chi-square was significant at 5 per cent level (value of Chi-square = 13.575 with P = .001<.05). So the null hypothesis was rejected, with a conclusion there is difference in the preference of Story element to attract the viewers in Malayalam film industry.

5) There is no difference in the marketing problems of Cine Exhibitors who concentrate on films in Malayalam or inother languages.

Multiple discriminant analysis was applied to test the null hypothesis. It could be inferred that the Wilk's Lambda represented by Chi-square was significant. So, the null hypothesis was rejected with a conclusion that the marketing problems were different for exhibitors who concentrated on films in Malayalam and those who concentrated on films in other languages.

6) There is no difference in the methods used for promotion of films by the cine distributors in Malayalam film industry.

The Friedman test was applied to test the null hypothesis and it was found that the value of Friedman Chi-square was significant at 5 per cent level (value of Chi-square = 401.109 with $P = .000 < .05$). Therefore, the null hypothesis was rejected with a conclusion that the methods used for the promotion of Malayalam films by cine distributors were different.

7.4 Conclusions

1) Production Problems with regard to Difficulty in Obtaining Government Grants, Cast and Crew, Focus on Stardom, Copyright and Intellectual Property Rights, Difficulty in Identification and Obtaining of Sources of Fund, and Visual Effects Industry greatly affected producers having a partnership form of ownership in companies and these producers were found to have a production experience ranging between 11-15 years.

2) When the marketing problems of film producers such as Tax, Film Certification, Multiplex, Competition from Other Entertainment Sectors are considered, producers having a production experience of above 20years were found to be facing the problem more seriously, also, these producers were concentrating in both the production and the distribution of films as well. In addition to that, all these producers had a partnership form of ownership in the companies.

3) Piracy, another major marketing problem, greatly affected film producer having a partnership form of ownership in the companies with concentration in production only, and producers withproduction experience ranging between 11-15 years were found to be facing the problem severely.

4) When the marketing problems of film distributors, such as Tax and Competition from Other Entertainment Sectors were taken into account the distributors having an experience ranging between 11 -15 years were found to face the problem severely; also, these distributors were concentrating more in Malayalam movies.

5) From the studyit could be concluded that promotional tools used by film distributors such as Creative Banners, Partnerships, Events, and Guerilla Marketing were the most suitable for the promotion of film distributors concentrating in Tamil movies,while promotional tools such as Road Shows, Discussion in Media, Internet Blogs and Hoardings were most suitable for the promotion of film distributors concentrating in Hindi movies.

6) Promotional tools such as Creative banners, Partnerships, Events and Guerilla Marketing were found the most suitable for the promotion of films

for distributors having an experience in distribution ranging between 16 – 20 years, and promotional tools such as Road Shows, Discussion in Media, Internet Blogs and Hoardings were found the most suitable for the promotion of films for distributors having an experience in distribution ranging between 11– 15 years.

7) It could be inferred that promotional tools such as Road Shows, Discussion in Media, Internet Blogs and Hoardings were most suited for film distributors concentrating in adventure films.On the other hand Partnerships, Events and Guerilla Marketing were apt promotion tools for distributors concentrating in comedy movies, and, for the distribution of crime movies, Creative Banners were the best suited promotion tool.

8) When marketing problems of Cine Exhibitors, with regard to Tax, Association, Multiplex, Class of Theatre and Piracy were considered, the A Class theatre owners concentrating in the exhibition of Malayalam movieswere found to be facing the problems most seriously. In addition to that, all these exhibitors had above 20 years of exhibition experience.

9) When Cine Exhibitors' marketing problems such as Ticket Prices, Sharing of Profits, Promotion Problems, Difficulty in Identification and Obtaining of Sources of Fund and Difficulty in the Obtaining Government Grant are taken into account, exhibitors owning B Class theatres with concentration in Malayalam movies and experience ranging between 11-15 years were found tobe facing these problems severely in the industry.

10) When marketing problems of Cine Exhibitors, such as Digital Revolution and E-Ticketing were

considered,exhibitors owning B Class theatres with concentration in Malayalam movies and above 20 years of experience in film exhibition were found facing the problem more seriously.

11) From the study,it was concluded that the element 'Story' was the most important element that attracted the viewers to movies in theatres followed by Star Cast and Music. Also, the least important element that attracted the viewers to movies in theatres was Advertisement.

12) It could be concluded that Piracy was the most vital problem faced by cine exhibitors in Malayalam language, followed by Sharing of Profit and Digital Revolution, whereas Multiplex was the most important problem faced by cine exhibitors in other languages, followed by Ticket Prices and Difficulty in Obtaining Institutional Funds.

7.5 Recommendations

1) A major problem encountered by the Malayalam film industry as a whole is the increased cost incurred in movie production. Several strategies can be applied by the producers in the industry, inorder to keep the cost under control, which includeavoiding night shooting; avoiding shooting in major commercial areas, concentratingfilm shooting location in areas where governmentsare providing various tax shelters etc

2) The State Government as well as the Central Government in close association with various associations functioning in the industry must make producers aware of the various grants provided to the movies produced in the industry; also,the proper rules and procedures in the sanctioning of these funds must also be clearly explained.

3) Proper and effective training must be given to producers, script writers, actors, technicians and other interested parties in the industry, by the Central as well as Sate Governments, in collaborationwith various associations and film development corporations functioning in the industry, which will help in the generation of excellent works and also in curbing the piracy threat to a great extent.

4) With regard to the certification process of each and every movie produced in the industry, more transparency must be initiated by the C.B.F.C. In addition to that, the huge delay incurred and the various hidden costs in the process of certification must also be stopped, which ultimately leads to increase in the number of movies produced in the industry.

5) The producers, distributors and cine exhibitors functioning in the industry should be made aware about the various taxes incurred in movie production, distribution and exhibition, by the Government and other interested and experienced parties including NGOs. Proper and effective communication of tax shelters and the speedy solutions for tax grievances must also be initiated by these abovesaid parties, which can help in the speedy release of movies in the industry.

6) The cine exhibitors functioning in the industry must clearly identify the major elements that attract the viewers to movies in theatres. The major elements include Story, Star Cast, Music, Banner, Advertisement etc.So, in accordance with the changing interests of the audience, the cine exhibitors must also adopt changes whenever and wherever necessary. Also, these types of adoptions

help the exhibitors to fill the theatres before the commencement of each show.

7) There must be a transparent and specific criterion in grading various theatres in the industry into A class, B class and C class. Also, the criterion must be formulated only after hearing the arguments put forward byall the parties associated with film exhibition, production and distribution.

8) With regard to the copyright and intellectual property rights prevailing in the industry, proper education must be provided to the parties associated with it, which ultimately helps in reducing the high cost and time incurred in obtaining these rights. Also in addition to that the ammendments made in the laws must be communicated by the Government or other agencies on a continuous basis, to interested parties associated with the production and distribution of movies.

9) The prominent associations prevailing in the industry in close collaboration with the Government must make the audience aware about the vast electronic ticketing facilities available to the audience in the industry. In addition to that the complaints relating to the same must be redressed on a speedy basis.

10) The distributors functioning in the industry must be made aware about the major tools for the promotion and distribution of films, such as Road Shows, Internet Blogs, Hoardings, Creative Banners, Events, Partnerships, Guerilla Marketing, etc and the effective and proper use of these tools.

11) The parties associated with film production should be made aware about the latest visual effect technologies that are available in the market, in order to withstand the tough competition prevailing

in the market from other industries, especially from Hollywood and Bollywood. The proper identification of skilled professionals who can handle the work within the budgeted cost is also of great importance.

7.6 Scope for Further Research

1) Role of Film Development Corporations in the Promotion of the Film Industry.
2) Impact of Technological Innovations in the Film Industry.

Bibliography

Ababa Addis. (2016). For Ehiopians Mother India is Mother of All Bollywood Films, *The Hindu Sunday,* p.18.

Abel Richard. (1996). *Silent Film,* The Athlone Press, 194-198.

Agnani Betty & Henry Aray.(2008). *Subsidies and Awards in Movie Production,* University of Granada.

Ajith Kumar P.K. (2016). Mollywood Hails Court Order on Udta Punjab, *The Hindu,* p.2.

Allam Richard. (1999). *Projecting Illusions, Films Spectatorships and Expressions of Reality,* Cambridge University Press Releases, 49-56.

Anandan, S. (2016). Film Certification Board Plays Villain's Role, *The Hindu,* p.2.

Andy Field. (2010). *Discovering Statistics Using SAS Software,* 11-28.

Augustine Jose. (2006). *Flesher and Images,* 55-61.

Basu Anustup. (2010). *Bollywood in the Age of New Media,* Edinburgh University Press, 61-74.

Belton John. (1996). *Movies and Mass Culture,* 40-43.

Benegal Shayam. (2006). *A Door to Adoor,* South Asian Cinema Foundation, 21-32.

Bhowmik Someswar. (2009). *Cinema and Censorship the Politics of Control in India,* 1-6.

Braun Edward. (1969). *Meyeshold on Theatre,* Melhurn and Company Limited, 76-79.

Carney Raymond. (1986). *American Vision the Films of Prank Capra,* 271-275.

Chakraborty Sucheta. (2016). Everybody Loves Vincent, *The Hindu,* p. 11.

Cleve Bastian. (2006). *Film Production Management,* Focal Press Publication, 50-55.

Cohen Keith. (1979). *Film and Fiction the Dynamic Exchange,* Yale University Press, 90-93.

Cooper Darius. (2000). *The Cinema of Satyajit Ray Between Traditional and Modernity,* Cambridge University Press, 175-180.

Dabashi Hamid. (2008). *The Making of a Rebel Filmmaker,* 63-79.

Daftuar Swati. (2016). A Map with New Directions, *The Hindu Sunday Magazine,* p.9.

David Silverman (2010). *Quantitative Research,* Sage Publishers, 13-31.

Deleuze Gilles. (2005). *Deleuze Cinema,* 6-8.

Densham D.H. (1959). *The Constitution of Research Films,* Pergamon Press, 4-16.

Dix Andrew. (2011). *Beginning Film Studies,* 111-118.

Dundoo Devi Sangeetha (2016). A Makeover in Progress, *The Hindu,* p.10.

Easthope Antony. (1993). *Contemporary Film Theory,* 101-110.

Egan Kelsey. (2014). Film Productions Design and Case Studies of the Great Gatsby, *Elonn Journal of Undergraduate Researches in Communications,* Vol. 5, No. 1.

Erich Lechman., & George. (1998). *Theory of Point Estimation,* 11-22.

Fielding Raymond. (1971). *The Technique of Special Effects Cinematography,* 15-23.

Furstenaw Marc. (2010). *The Film Theory Readers Debates and Arguments,* 290-293.

Gabriel Karem. (2010). *Melodrama and the Nation, Sexual Economies of Bombay Cinema 1970-2000,* 69-88.

Gera Anjali. (2012). *The Magic of Bollywood at Home and Abroad, Sage Publications,* India Pvt. Linited, 69-78.

Gokulsing Moti., & Dissanayake Wimal. (2000). *Indian Popular Cinema- A Narrative of Cultural Change,* Orient Longman Publication, 56-94.

GokulsingMoti., & Dissanayake Wimal.(1988). *Indian Popular Cinema- A Narrative of Cultural Change,* Baba Barkha Nath Press, New Delhi, 117-120.

Gopinath Swapna., & Raj Jalarajan Sony. (2015). Gender Construct as Narrative and Text: The Female Protagonists in New Generation Malayalam Cinema, *South Asian Popular Culture.*

Harbord Janet. (2002). *Film Cultures,* Sage Publication, 48-52.

Hood John.(2009). *The Essential Mystery Major Filmmakers of Indian art Cinema,* 9-15.

Ibkar Alisha. (2015). The Natyasastras and Indian Cinemas: A Study of Rasa Theory as a Cornerstone for Indian Aesthetics, *International Journal of English Languages & Translation Studies,* pp.80-87.

Indraganti Krishna Mohana.(2016). Faith in the Formula Film, *The Hindu,* p.9.

Jha Somesh. (2016). Cinema Halls May Soon Work 24/7, *The Hindu,* p. 16.

Joseph Hair. (2010). *Multivariate Data Analysis,* Pearson Publication, 2-16.

Joseph Merin. (2016). The Super-hero Stereotypes and Post-modernist Woes, *The Hindu,* p.14.

Joshi Namrata. (2016). Canvases on Celluloid, *The Hindu,* p.11.

Joshi Namrata. (2016). Letting Our Films Fly, *The Hindu Daily,* p.9.

Joshi Namrata. (2016). Nothing Queer about Gay Films, *The Hindu Daily,* p.13.

K Bhumika. (2016). Predominant Voice in Cinema Still that of Men, *The Hindu,* p.9.

Kaur Raminder & Sinha Ajay. (2000). *Bollywood Popular Indian Cinema through a Transnational Lens,* Sage Publication, New Delhi, 14-18.

Kavoori Anandan., & Punathambekar Aswin.(2009). *Global Bollywood,* Oxford University Press, 7-10.

Kazmi Fareed. (1999). *The Politics of India's Conventional Cinema,* Sage Publication, New Delhi, 79-87.

Khajane Muralidhara. (2016). Censor Board is Often Misused by Party in Power, *The Hindu,* p.9.

Khan Zara. (2016). Netflix So What, *The Hindu Sunday Magazine,* p.1.

Kidiyoor Gururaj, Yatgiri Prashant; & Shetty Ranjan Sham. (2015). *Kannada Film Industry Challenges and the Way Forward,* Karnataka Chalanchitra Academy.

Kumar Krishna, Kumar Ajith. (2016). Monsoon Surprise at Box Office, *The Hindu Sunday Edition,* p.2.

Kumar Naresh. (1995). *Indian Cinema Ebbs and Tides,* Har-Anand Publication, New Delhi, 17-23.

Kumar Pranab. (1986). *Contemporary Text Book on Statistical Analysis,* 480-549.

Kumar Rajinder. (2006). *Sociology Goes to the Movies,* Sage Publications, 15-31.

Labato Ramon. (2012). *Shadow Publications,* 11-15.

Lent John. (1990). *The Asian Film Industry,* Christopher Helm Publishing Company, 55-59.

Liese.,& Klaus. (2008). *Statistical Decision Theory,* 21-34.

Mamer Bruce. (2000). *Film Production Technique Creating the Accomplished Image,* 16-31.

Mark J. (1987). *Review of Multivariate Analysis,* 391-411.

MathurMeera; & Goswami Shubham.(2012). A Study of Consumers Behavior and Product Palacement in Indian Cinema, *Annals of Management Research,* Volume 2, No 1.

Mazumdar Ranjani. (2007). *Bombay Cinema an Archie of the City,* 45-52.

Mohan Jag. (1984). *S. Sukhdev Film Maker- A Documentary Montage,* 99-116.

Mohan Jag. (1990). *Documentary Film and Indian Awakening,* Publication Division, 35-37.

Mukherjee Akaitab. (2014). Theory of Indian Cinema, International Journal of English, Language, *Journal and Humanities,* Volume II, Issue VII, November 2014.

Mulvey Laura. (1975). *Visual Pleasures and Narrative Cinema, Film Psychology, Society and Ideology.*

Nagarajan Saraswathy. (2016). Lights Camera Action, Friday Review Arts and Culture, *The Hindu,* p.1.

NathDivesh. (2016). Art of Visual Storytelling.Education Plus, *The Hindu Sunday,* p.4.

Nazeer Mohamed. (2015). An Unsound Trend in Mollywood, *The Hindu Daily,* p.13.

Neu Timm. (2007).Bollywood is coming Copyright and Film Industry Issues Regarding International Film

Co-Productions Involving India, Cornell Law School Graduate Student Papers.

Nicholas Bill. (2010). *Engaging Cinema an Introduction to Film Studies,* 150-156.

Noonan Keith. (2016). 3 Trends That Will Shape the Movie Industry in 2016, *The Motley Fool,* p.11-16.

Oommen, M.A, Joseph, K.V. (1990). *Economics of Indian Cinema,* C-DIT Series, 14-19.

Ouyang Chun, HofstedeTer Arthur, Rosa La Marcello, Rosemann Michael. (2008). *Camera, Set, Action Automating Film Production via Business Process Management,* p.1.

Parayil Kumar Sujith. (2014). *Synoptique —An Online Journal of Film and Moving Images Studies.*

Park James. (1984). *Learning to Dream the New British Cinema,* Faber and Faber Publishers, London, 53-61.

Peter J. (2001). *Mathematical Statistics,* 16-38.

Praveen, M.P. (2016). When Mollywood Trailers Steal the Show, *The Hindu,* p.2.

Rabiger Michael. (2004). *Directing the Documentary,* Panchsheel Garden, 23-68.

Rajadhyaksha Ashish. (2009). *Indian Cinema in Time of Celluloid from Bollywood to the Emergency,* 10-13.

RamachandranNaman. (2016). We Get High on Cinema, *The Hindu Sunday Magazine,* p.1.

Raman Giji. (2016). Giving a Kung Fu Punch to Films, *The Hindu,* p.2.

Rangan Baradwaj. (2016). Back to Blaming the Movies, *The Hindu,* p.9.

Rangan Baradwaj. (2016). Moving Images Moving Words. *The Hindu Sunday Magazine,* p. 3.

Rangan Baradwaj. (2016). Small Film – Metaphysical Weight, *The Hindu Sunday Magazine,* p.3.

Rangan Baradwaj. (2016).If Rushes were Horses, Screening Room, *The Hindu,* p.3.

Rao Mohit. (2016). Romas go to Bollywood, *The Hindu Sunday Magazine,* p.2.

Ray Satyajit. (1976). *Our Films Their Films,* Oxford Printing Press, 21-72.

Robert Torrie. (1977). *Principles and Procedures of Statistics,* 22-36.

Robinson, M.N. (1939). *The Film Answers Book,* Great Britain Press, 45-48.

Rothman William. (2004). *The I of the Camera,* 2-10.

Sarkar Kabita. (1975). *Indian Cinema Today an Analysis,* Sterling Publishers Private Limited, 110-116.

Sen Aditi. (2016). Putting up a Good Fight, *The Hindu,* p.11.

Sexena Ambrish. (2004). *Indian Cinema Society and Culture,* Kanishka Publishers, New Delhi, 16-19.

Shahani Parmesh. (2015). Mumbai the Ultimate Jugaad City, *The Hindu Newspaper,* p.16.

Shingler Martin. (2012). *Star Studio a Critical Guide,* Polgrave Manmillian Publication, 40-47.

Srinivas S.V. (2009). *Megastar Chiranjeevi and Telugu Cinema after NT Rama Rao,* Oxford University Press, New Delhi, 16-23.

Stapes Donald. (1973). *The American Cinema,* New York University, 1-8.

Steven Peter. (1985). *Jump Cut Hollywood Politics and Counter Cinema,* 63-68.

Stiglerr, Stephen M. (1978). *Mathematical Statistics in Early States,* 190-216.

Stishova Yelena. (1989). *Look Who's Here: A New Trend in the Soviet Cinemas,* Panchsheel Publishers, 22-46.

Swann Pau. (1987). *The Hollywood Films in Post War Britain,* CroomHelm Publications, 61-64.

Turner Graeme. (1988). *Film as Social Practice,* Routledge Press, 29-38.

Turner Graeme. (1999). *Film as a Social Practice,* Routledge Taylor and Francis Group, 47-50.

Turok Ivan. (2003). *Cities, Clusters and Creative Industry: A Case of Films and Televisions in Scotland,* European Planning Studies, Vol. 11, No. 5.

Vasudev Aruna. (1978). *Liberty and Licence in the Indian Cinema,* Vikas Publications, 2-10.

Vasudevan Rani. (2010). *The Melodramatic Public Film Forms and Spectatorship in Indian Cinema,* Permanent Black Publication, 16-31.

Vitali Valentina.,&Willemen Paul. (2006). *Theorising National Cinema,* Palgrave Macmillian Publication, 17-26.

Wagner Robert. (1975). *The Education of the Film Maker an International View,* The UNESCO Press, 30-34.

Wald, Abraham. (1947). *Sequential Analysis,* 18-57.

Walter Ernest. (1969). *Film Cutting Room,* Focal Press, London, 16-31.

Watkins Beth. (2016). *Two Moods of Bengali Cinema,* The Hindu, p.11.

Woods Jeanie. (2011). *Vision of Empires and others Imagining Cinemas of Ireland and India, 1910-1962,* 28-36.

■■■■■